AF454305

HOW TO SURVIVE IN
BABYLON

COURTNEY SHARPE

This book is dedicated to those navigating
the everyday struggle.

CONTENTS

ACKNOWLEDGMENTS

———

I want to start by thanking my cousin, who introduced me to the person that inspired me to write this book. That moment was the beginning of everything.

Thank you to everyone who gave feedback on my work. Your insights were invaluable in shaping the final version.

A special thanks to Kelvin from KayVee Books, whose expertise transformed my manuscript into a polished book ready for print. Your support made all the difference.

INTRODUCTION

In this book, you'll often come across the word "Babylon." You might wonder, what does Babylon mean? In this introduction, I'll give you a brief summary of what I mean by Babylon today, not the historical context from where it originally came.

The Babylon I'm talking about is a systematic program we all know as the government. Babylon is a system with its own institutions, like schools, hospitals, banks, and so on. The media, news, and corporate television are also part of the Babylon system.

Babylon isn't just a system; it's also a society. It's become a way of life for the modern Western world. This society reflects what the Babylon system stands for: chaos, confusion, and disorder.

Part I

SURVIVING IN BABYLON

CHAPTER 1

———

HOW TO MOVE IN BABYLON

Surviving in Babylon these days is tough with everything happening around us daily. You might wonder how to navigate a society that's so rigid, stuck in its ways, and unwilling to take responsibility for its actions. We face peer pressure from friends, societal trends, the struggle between being popular and not, constant political agendas affecting everyday life, broken families, distractions from celebrities and social media, identity issues like gender confusion, and the list goes on.

You might ask, how can anyone succeed in a society with so many obstacles? Let's start with some basic principles for navigating Babylon.

#1 - Know Yourself

First, you must know who you are. Without self-knowledge, you can't be consistent in your daily actions, which will leave you feeling complacent. To know who you are, start your journey of self-discovery. This will help you understand how you function as an individual. Ask yourself: What are your likes and dislikes? What motivates you to get things done? What type of people do you enjoy being around? Who do you prefer to avoid?

Can you be yourself around different kinds of people? If the answer is yes, that's great. If the answer is no, let's take a basic approach to change that. First, study the different types of people around you. Then, find a part of their personality or lifestyle that resonates with you and use that to build common ground.

Knowing yourself also means accepting yourself. Many people struggle with this due to what I call a character diversion. This is when someone diverts their true character and behaves with a false sense of self. This isn't healthy, as it creates a psychological barrier in your mind. For example, if you act out of character to fit into a certain social circle, you'll start to believe the real you isn't good enough for that circle. This can create self-doubt and make you question your decisions, stagnating your growth and building unhealthy frustration. Therefore, it's very important to be yourself without apologies. Remember, to be yourself is to know yourself.

#2 - Think For Yourself

To navigate Babylon effectively, you have to think for yourself. This can be challenging, as many people tend not to think independently due to social engineering from social media, TV, peers, and even parents and social circles. Receiving information from others and keeping an open mind isn't a problem. However, if you accept information without questioning it, that can cause issues in the long run. Incorrect information can lead to bad decisions that might have irreversible consequences.

One way to think for yourself is to educate yourself on various subjects. This can change your mindset and help you understand the world and society better. Knowing how people operate will help you move effectively. Let's look at some examples of how you can navigate Babylon effectively.

First and foremost, If you're travelling to work on public transport, like a bus or train, instead of listening to music or watching a video on your phone, take a few minutes to look around. Observe the behaviour of the people around you, see how they interact with each other, and notice how they move. If you do this every time you use public transport, you'll start to see patterns of behaviour.

For instance, on your bus journey, you might notice that most people are anti-social, just sitting on their phones and not engaging with each other. If this is a regular occurrence, you'll learn that your bus ride to work isn't the best place to try and socialise. Most people on that journey just want to be on their phones and aren't interested in socialising. This observation will teach you how to navigate public transport more effectively.

Secondly, Make it a daily habit to study your environment every time you step outside, whether you're just going to the shop, taking a walk, heading to work on public transport, or attending an event. In today's modern society, there are many different characters, and understanding this helps you navigate through the everyday chaos of Babylon.

For example, whenever you walk in public, use what I call the 180-degree look-around view. This means looking straight ahead, then to your left, back to straight ahead, then to your right, and back to straight ahead again. This practice helps you see what's happening on both sides of you, increasing your awareness.

It's important to understand that many unstable people are walking around in public daily, so being aware of your surroundings helps you move accordingly. Consistently studying your environment keeps you ahead of the average person. It allows you to see how people interact with each other and how they react to situations. This type of awareness prepares you to deal with different types of people and successfully navigate your everyday environment.

Finally, We live in a society that's often uncivil, hostile, and sometimes even violent. One reason for this is that many people don't know how to respond calmly and effectively. So, let's briefly discuss how to move with inner peace in Babylon society.

When you step outside, programme your mind to be at peace. If you don't know how to do this, here's a simple approach: Tell yourself, "As I leave my house today, I will not commit violence, I will not argue with anyone, I will not react but only respond, I will not cause any problems, I will just go about my business and come home in one piece." Operating with this mindset and attitude will help you deal better with people, including the hostile ones you might encounter in public or at work.

For instance, if someone accidentally bumps into you but apologises because they're in a rush, instead of reacting angrily, respond calmly and say, "It's okay." This way, you save your energy and go about your day without added stress.

#3 - Build Your Confidence

Confidence is another principle that will help you not only survive in Babylon but also lead a prosperous life wherever you are in the world. In a society that doesn't really encourage individuality, it can be hard to be confident in yourself and your abilities. Many people behave like clones of each other, lacking originality and too afraid to be themselves. They lack the courage and confidence to show their true character.

If you continue to live without confidence, it will hinder your growth and progress. You might become jealous of those around you who have the confidence to pursue their goals while you just stand by and watch them flourish. This jealousy can build up in your heart because you wish you had their confidence.

But what if I told you that you can be just as confident as your peers? You might ask, how can I get to that level of confidence? Let's explore some examples of how to build confidence in yourself.

Firstly, try stepping outside of your comfort zone and doing something you've never done before. This can reveal a side of yourself you didn't know existed. For example, if you're used to going to events with friends and have never gone alone, try going to an event by yourself. See if you have the confidence to socialise without your friends by your side. If you accomplish this, you'll notice a boost in your confidence to do more things on your own. This will also build your character and create self-confidence.

Another way to build confidence is to speak your mind. When you do this, make sure you do it with caution and good communication skills so that people can understand and digest what you're saying. Speaking your mind is a liberating experience that money can't buy—it's a priceless gift from life itself. However, it does come with a cost that you must be willing to accept and acknowledge.

Speaking your mind might lead to falling out with friends, family, or other people you know or associate with. So, be cautious, but not fearful. I understand that for many, speaking your mind can be very difficult because you're used to being passive and not saying what you really need to say, which isn't healthy. Let's look at a three-step process to make speaking your mind a natural part of your life.

Step 1: Try speaking your mind throughout an entire day while interacting with people. Start with someone you know and see how you get on.

Step 2: If you were successful on the first day, keep going. Add an extra day each time until you reach a full week of speaking your mind.

Step 3: Now that you've completed steps 1 and 2, it's time to assess the impact. Ask yourself: How do you feel about completing this task? What impact did it have on your life? Is there anything you could have done better to get better results?

Step 4: Now comes the real challenge. The first three steps were just the start, preparing you for a new lifestyle. In this final step, make steps 1-3 a regular part of your daily life. Trust the process, and you'll see the benefits.

This approach is great for those who are usually passive and want to become more assertive and direct. It will help increase your confidence and strengthen your character.

Another strategy for surviving in Babylon is to move in complete silence. Many people find this difficult in today's social media era, where everyone wants to be seen, heard, and noticed for everything they do. Some even share their personal issues, family problems, and other woes online. Exposing yourself like this on social media isn't wise, as many people don't have your best interests at heart. Also, remember that anything you post can be used against you if you're not careful. The exception is if you're promoting a business or services that benefit you and others.

Moving in silence helps keep the spotlight off you while you pursue your goals. It allows you to focus more because no one knows your moves.

#4 - Move Strategically

To survive in Babylon, it's important to move very strategically. Acting wild, reckless, or random isn't a good practice. It's not wise to let people predict your every move, as some may not have your best interests at heart and might try to block your progress out of jealousy and envy. Often, it's those closest to you who can hinder your success.

One key practice is not revealing every move you make. A common mistake is putting too much trust in people, especially those we've known for a long time. We often think we can trust "best friends" a hundred percent, but only realise their true nature when we fall out with them. You might have shared your darkest secrets with someone, and if you fall out, they could use that information against you. So, be careful and strategic about how much you reveal, regardless of how close you are.

Moving strategically brings order and organisation to your life, especially in a society where many people lack structure and wonder why success eludes them. Moving strategically means thinking ahead, allowing you to make necessary plans for success. Many people live by the acronym Y.O.L.O (You Only Live Once), which is true but must be understood in context. You only live once, meaning you only get one chance to get it right, make the most of your life, create a foundation for your family, and leave a legacy.

Moving strategically can help you put the Y.O.L.O concept into proper practice. Let's look at a few examples of how to implement strategical movement in your life to succeed.

Let's say you want to have a productive week, now remember, you only have seven days to work with. Start on Sunday by writing a to-do list of what you want to achieve for the week. Once you've done that, begin the process the very next day. Don't worry if you don't accomplish everything on your list. Just make sure to tick off what you have achieved and carry over any unfinished tasks to the following week. This strategy is great for achieving goals within a certain timeframe. It helps maintain a steady flow of progress and makes you feel good about yourself, knowing that you are moving forward.

Another example is to be organised. Organisation is a great strategy that helps maintain a steady level of movement in your life. Being organised keeps your mind clear, which in turn helps you maintain a clear vision of what you need to do. A clear vision allows you to determine whether your goals are realistic. To move in an orderly manner, you must be organised in your thoughts, vision, and actions.

For example, look at your home and ask yourself, "Is my house in order?" If the answer is yes, that's great. If not, it's something you need to fix. Start by keeping everything in its place. This helps you function properly at home and makes it easier to find things when you need them. It creates a steady flow of organised movement. Practice putting things back where you found them instead of leaving them in random places around your home.

Thirdly, structure is another important strategy to have in your life. It brings order and is a form of discipline that aligns with your strategy. Structure and strategy go hand in hand. Without structure, your life can become chaotic, and you might find that nothing gets done at the start or end of each day. If you live like this daily, you'll end up with wasted days, weeks, months, and possibly years with nothing to show for your time on earth. This isn't something to be proud of.

A basic level of structure can be as simple as going to the gym three times a week, going for a jog a few days a week, or doing a deep clean of your house every month. These are just basic examples of how to maintain order in your life.

When moving around in everyday Babylon society, it's important to be quiet, humble, and cautious. One of the biggest mistakes people make today is exposing too much of themselves, whether on social media or in public. For example, some people like to show off their material possessions, like their car, their house, or their luxurious lifestyle on social media. This behaviour only creates jealousy and is unwise in a world where many people are struggling to get by.

Another strategy is to move in disguise—blend in with society and avoid bringing too much attention to yourself. Have you heard of the term "hidden in plain sight"? Sometimes you need to guard your true intentions around people you don't know. This doesn't mean pretending to be something you're not;

it means not being quick to open up or show off your wealth. Many of the richest people dress casually and avoid flashy jewellery, giving the impression of being average while hiding their true wealth. This keeps the spotlight off them.

The lesson here is to be comfortable in who you are and let your character speak for itself. If you struggle to be comfortable in your own skin, you might need to look inside yourself and ask why you feel such discomfort with your character.

In a society where many people are struggling financially just to make ends meet, it's important to understand their mindset so you can move accordingly. For those surviving on an average job salary or government benefits in low-income areas, life is about survival. If you live in such areas, the effective strategy is to move as if you're poor. This doesn't mean you should leave your house looking homeless or neglecting your appearance. What I mean is to avoid being too flashy and driving expensive cars in low-income neighbourhoods where people may not have much, even though they might try to portray a false image of wealth.

It's about being aware of the society you live in and understanding that not everyone around you is doing well. You may not be aware of their struggles because they keep their problems to themselves. The key to this strategy is to remain as low-key as possible about your lifestyle, especially if you are doing well among people who are not. In other words, be mindful of those around you before sharing any information about yourself.

#5 - Stay Grounded

To thrive and survive in a Babylonian society, you need to stay grounded. Being grounded means being at peace with yourself, understanding the ever-changing reality around you, showing empathy to others, and looking out for more than just yourself. It means having balanced views on life and maintaining inner peace. In a society like this, you might wonder how to keep yourself grounded. Let's look at some examples of how to do just that.

Firstly, try to appreciate the simple things in life that you might take for granted, like just being able to breathe every day. Be grateful that you wake up to see another day and appreciate the fresh air you breathe.

Secondly, appreciate that you can afford to eat every day, as there are people in the world who struggle to meet this basic need.

Thirdly, be thankful for your physical mobility to walk around every day. While this might be normal for most of us, there are people in wheelchairs or those who need walking sticks and lack this mobility.

Fourthly, it's important to appreciate the important things you already have in your life right now. Often, we focus on what we don't have and compare ourselves to others, sometimes even watching the lives of celebrities on reality TV. These shows are popular because people wish to live the flashy lifestyles they see. But in reality, those celebrities aren't as happy as they seem. They live their lives on camera, with paparazzi following them around, and fans who only love them for their fame. This isn't genuine love. Celebrities can't walk around freely without security because their net worth is broadcasted to the world, making them targets. Their lifestyle isolates them from reality and distorts their sense of it. They aren't free to move as they want —they're like rich slaves, trapped in a world far removed from everyday life. So, even if you don't have the riches of celebrities, be grateful you can walk around freely without worrying about being a target. Appreciate that people can like you for your character, not for what you have.

Finally, be open and willing to learn from others. Listen to different viewpoints, not just your own. Don't be quick to react just because someone's opinion differs from yours. Teach yourself to listen first, then respond after you've heard what they have to say. This approach helps you have a balanced view of life and see things from different perspectives, increasing your understanding of how real life works and why people behave the way they do. This balance is key to staying grounded in a society that often has one-sided views.

These five examples are just basic ways to ground yourself in a society full of vanity, chaos, disorder, toxicity, and other forms of destruction detrimental to human nature.

#6 - Self Acceptance

For this principle, we'll discuss self-acceptance and not trying to fit in. Most of us were told at least once in our lives that we should try to fit in with our peers. But what does it really mean to fit in? Is there such a thing as fitting in? If there is, how do you go about doing it, and at what cost?

Let's explore how people today in Western society try to fit in. For example, imagine you're the new kid in school. You see all the kids playing football, bonding through the game. But you don't like football. Do you try to play, even though you're not good at it and don't enjoy it, just to fit in? Or do you accept that football isn't your thing and not waste your time?

What if you start a new job and during lunch in the staff room, everyone is talking about football, but you're not into it at all? If a colleague asks you which team you support, will you be honest and say you don't watch football, or will you pretend to support a team to fit in?

Think back to when you were a teenager and your friends tried smoking. Did you take a puff to look cool and gain acceptance, or did you refuse because you knew it wasn't a healthy habit? At some point, we've all felt the pressure to fit in. Many of us fall into the trap of trying to fit into a society that dictates how we should act, behave, and follow popular trends without question.

The idea of fitting in is a false concept created by Western society to make us believe we can fit in with people who don't share our interests. Even if we have something in common, it doesn't mean we truly fit in. Why do you think some people who fail to fit in suffer from mental health issues or low self-esteem? Why is depression at an all-time high? It's because people are trying to fit into a part of society that's impossible to fit into. To fit in would imply that everyone is the same, but we're not. So, how does one really fit in? The answer is: nowhere. Nobody fits in anywhere.

The only place you fit in is within yourself, which leads to self-acceptance. Self-acceptance is a key principle to live by if you are to survive in a Babylonian society where most people refuse to accept themselves. They don't know how because they haven't been taught, due to the heavy social engineering of Western society. Some people may ask, "How do I accept myself?" Let's look at some basic ways to achieve self-acceptance.

Scenario 1: Your friends want to go out to a club and invite you along. You know that going to the club isn't really your thing, but you worry about how your friends will perceive you if you tell them you don't want to go. This puts you in a dilemma. The simple solution is to just tell them no and that you're not interested in going to the club. Accept the fact that clubbing isn't your thing, and don't be afraid to let your friends know so they can stop asking you to go.

Scenario 2: Let's say you're in an environment where people like to wear flashy designer clothes. You feel that to fit in, you must also wear flashy designer clothes. However, you don't care for designer clothes and have no desire to wear them because you're happy with standard labels. If you're not a flashy, flamboyant person, then accept that about yourself and don't worry about how others view you.

Scenario 3: You may come from a religious family, heavily involved in the church. As an adult, you've decided to live by different morals and principles that don't align with your family's religious beliefs. Are you going to pretend to follow your family's religious ways, or will you accept your own way of living that makes you happy and content? The best approach is to accept yourself as a non-religious person because that's how you're currently living, and if it makes you happy, then it's something you should accept as your way of life, plain and simple.

#7 - Be Original

Be original—this principle is all about embracing your uniqueness. When you look around society, do you see originality, or do you see clones and carbon copies of people mimicking one another? Think about that question, as it's an interesting one to ponder.

To be original means to have your own mind, your own sense of direction, and your own vision of how you want to live your life. It means finding your own way and not copying what someone else is doing. Being original also means embracing who you are unapologetically, without doubting or questioning your character. Remember, there's only one version of you, and no one else can truly mimic you. So why not embrace your unique character? Why not accept who you are? Why try to be a clone of someone else when you can be your own unique self?

The importance of being original lies in understanding that you have a unique character to bring to society. You may have a different perspective on the world based on your vision, mindset, and attitude towards life. Being original means you bring something to the world no one else can—not because you're special, but because your character is different from everyone else's.

Trying to be a clone of someone else is detrimental to the growth of your character. Without understanding originality, some might think copying someone else's character will yield the same results, which is absolutely false. The fact that many people think this way is concerning. A society full of clones doesn't progress; it creates dysfunction, depression, self-hate, internal chaos, character disorientation, suicide, identity crises and more.

Let's explore a few ways to embrace your originality:

(i) Be around people who accept you for who you are

It's important to be around people who accept you as you are because it helps you to accept yourself, which is very healthy for your well-being. When your surroundings embrace you for who you are, you don't have to pretend to be something you're not. This boosts your confidence to be your original self and helps you thrive in your unique character.

(ii) Spend quality time with yourself every day

Spending quality time with yourself is important as it grounds you in your thoughts, feelings, and overall vision of where you're going in life. If you're constantly around people and never make time for yourself, your mind can get overwhelmed by different voices, opinions, and outlooks on life from others. This can cause you to lose your own sense of direction. Spending time with yourself allows you to stay true to your original state of being, which is beneficial for maintaining your originality.

(iii)Take time to evaluate your character.

Taking time to evaluate your character is a good practice. This helps you calculate your moves in life, check in with yourself, and find ways to improve and add value to yourself. Self-evaluation ensures you are in alignment with yourself and heading in the right direction. If you feel like you're losing yourself amidst life's turbulences, it's time to take a break and evaluate your character. Always remember to evaluate yourself at least once a month.

(iv) Listen to your inner voice

Listening to your inner voice can be very helpful in navigating society. Often, we ignore that intuitive voice inside us, sometimes referred to as our gut feeling or instinct. Ignoring this guiding voice can be a big mistake. We must learn to trust our inner voice more, as it is a crucial part of who we are inside.

(v) Occasionally go into a state of solitude.

To stay in tune with yourself and aligned with your character, it's important to go into a state of solitude from time to time. Don't be afraid to be alone sometimes; it's good to escape the noise and distractions of society. This doesn't mean completely cutting yourself off from people. Going into solitude means giving yourself a better chance to know yourself, which allows you to be more original in your character. This practice aligns well with the principle of being your original self.

CHAPTER 2

STUDYING THE SYSTEM IN BABYLON

One of the key principles for surviving in Babylon is to study the system you're a part of. Many people don't take the time to learn how the system works, often because they find politics boring or think it doesn't concern them. This kind of thinking is why many end up making bad decisions that affect them later on.

For example, someone might buy a house and go through all the legal steps, feeling accomplished because they're on the property ladder. But here's the catch: if you haven't finished paying off your mortgage and start missing payments, you risk losing your home to repossession. What the homeowner might not have considered is that inflation keeps rising, which drives up the cost of living. This is a systemic issue we all face and have little control over. If your salary doesn't increase to match the rising costs, how will you keep up with your mortgage payments in the future?

Additionally, the land your house is built on belongs to the government. If they decide they need that land for any reason, they have the right to take it, even if the house is legally yours. Many people aren't aware of this because they don't take the time to understand how the system works.

Studying the system helps you make better-informed decisions for your future because it allows you to anticipate the political climate of your country and adjust your actions accordingly. Understanding the system lets you see how it impacts your daily life and future, giving you insight into how to plan ahead. It also helps you know your rights and what you're entitled to within the system you're a part of.

Knowing the system means understanding the political conditions that affect your everyday life, which gives you an advantage. You might wonder why you should bother learning about the system. The answer is simple: it's in your best interest. When you know how the system works, you can plan your life more effectively, make informed decisions for yourself and your family, and become more financially literate.

For example, if you're aware that the cost of living is going to rise due to inflation, you're in a better position to start thinking about your finances and how to manage your money. The Babylon system we live in controls the working environment, and affects the society we live in, the schools our children attend, the banks, the supermarkets, and every other establishment in the Western world. If you don't take the time to understand the system you live under, you'll likely fall behind as its effects catch up with you.

The system we live in isn't designed for us to thrive—it's built to keep most people in a subservient position while the top one percent (1%) reap the benefits. To survive and thrive in this system, it's crucial to understand how it works so you don't get taken advantage of.

To understand the system, there are certain aspects you need to study. Let's take a brief look at what you should focus on:

- Look into how politics affects your daily life.
- Understand how politics influences your working environment.
- See how politics impacts the way schools operate.
- Consider how politics shapes what your children learn in school.
- Examine how politics affects your living environment.
- Understand how politics influences the cost of living.
- Observe how politics controls the narrative of news

broadcasts.
- Consider how politics shapes the mindset of everyday people.
- Study how politics runs the country and treats the people it governs.
- Read books about politics to gain a deeper understanding of the system.

These points are just a few ways to start learning about the system. Almost every organisation or establishment is connected to it in some way. The conclusion here is that the system controls our daily lives, whether we realise it or not. So, it's crucial to understand how it works, how it affects us, and how we can make the system work for us.

By not studying the system, you risk becoming a victim of its constant pressures, like the rising cost of living and the relentless media narrative. Many people struggle in society because they lack knowledge of how their decisions will affect them later on, especially at a systematic level. That's why it's important to study the rules of the system so you can be better prepared, make smarter decisions, and become more financially literate, avoiding the trap of just working to pay bills.

CHAPTER 3

HOW TO THINK IN BABYLON

One of the key principles for surviving in Babylon is about how you think. Critical thinking is essential in a society where many people don't think for themselves. Some might ask, "How am I supposed to think?" It's not so much about how to think, but rather how to develop the ability to think for yourself.

Philosophically speaking, it starts with not just accepting what you're told. Always question the information you're given. If you don't have knowledge about a certain subject, it's important to do your own research to fully understand it, rather than relying on someone else's interpretation. Being around people who challenge your thinking can also help. When someone challenges your thought process, it's not always an attack on your mindset. Sometimes, our thinking isn't correct, so we need to challenge ourselves to improve.

To survive in Babylon, it's crucial to think on a revolutionary level, as revolution means bringing about change. Develop a thought process that can change your life and circumstances. To get ahead in Babylon, your thinking needs to be unorthodox, going against the usual way of thinking. You need to raise your thinking to a higher standard; average thinking won't get you very far in a system like the one we have today.

The current system has plans and agendas that were set in motion years before they surfaced. The system is always years ahead, while many of us only think about today, and barely consider tomorrow. This is because our minds have been trained to think short-term, rather than long-term.

Our minds have been systematically programmed to think

short-term, which is why many of us only achieve short-term results instead of long-term success. The goal should be to start thinking long-term. For example, many of us try to escape our harsh realities by going on expensive holidays, spending a lot of money, only to return to the same situation we were trying to escape from. This often leads to feeling depressed again because our current conditions haven't changed. That's what I call short-term results—you go on holiday for a week or two, have a great time, experience a temporary high, then come back home and feel down again, repeating this cycle year after year without any real change.

This is what I call insanity—doing the same thing over and over while expecting different results. The long-term approach would be to sit down and think about creating a life that you don't need to escape from. Ask yourself: What kind of life do you want in the long term? What kind of person do you aspire to be in the long term? Where do you want to be in life in the long term? What legacy do you want to leave on earth before you die?

Do you see the pattern in these questions? They're designed to get you thinking long-term instead of just living in the moment. Many of us get caught up in our feelings and make short-term, emotionally driven decisions without considering their long-term impact. We focus on how we feel right now, which isn't a good habit. Let's explore some examples of how you can develop a long-term mindset.

#1 - Make the Most of Your Week

You have 7 days in a week, so instead of just coasting through each day, take a moment to ask yourself what you'd like to achieve during that time. Once you've figured out what you want to accomplish in those seven days, start working on it day by day to reach your goal for the week.

#2 - Prioritise Needs Over Wants

Let's say you're thinking about buying a few expensive items. Now, pause and ask yourself: do you really need these items, or do you simply want them? If you don't need them, perhaps they can wait. This is the time to think long-term. What's more important for your future—what you want right now, or what you need that will benefit you in the long run? The lesson here is to prioritise what will truly benefit you in the future, rather than just satisfying a temporary desire.

#3 - Choose Long-Term Value

Always put your wants last and your needs first. Your needs are what truly matter, while your wants are often short-term desires. Think of it this way: your wants represent short-term thinking, while your needs reflect long-term thinking. By consistently prioritising your needs over your wants, you'll develop a habit of long-term thinking.

For example, instead of buying an expensive item you want but don't really need, you could invest that money in a book on financial literacy. This could benefit you in the long term by teaching you how to manage your money better, whereas the costly item wouldn't offer the same lasting value.

Critical thinking is an essential tool for navigating a society where this type of thinking is often lacking. To use critical thinking effectively, you need to approach life with analytical skills, logic, and the ability to identify the root causes of problems and find solutions. It's also important to ask questions and remain non-reactive. Being a critical thinker means thinking first before reacting; living in a constant state of reactivity can be harmful, as it often leads to poor decisions that can't be undone. This is why it's crucial to think logically and rationally.

We live in a society that is very reactive, which is why there's so much chaos and disorder. To raise a generation of critical thinkers, this process must begin at an early age in the home. Unfortunately, the Babylon system doesn't teach critical thinking —not in schools or any other educational institutions. Instead, it bombards you with information that doesn't challenge the brain to think, leading to intellectual laziness.

It's important to keep your brain sharp and active by reading, researching, and being open to learning new things that encourage forward-thinking. In today's society, there's a common mentality of living for the moment and dealing with the consequences later. For example, trying to live a lifestyle you can't afford is driven by the thought process of "if I look rich, people will treat me with respect," which is far from the truth. This mentality is often pushed onto people in society.

Instead, we need to upgrade our level of thinking. Rather than focusing on impressing others with our physical appearance, we should strive to be better people, improve our character, and think about how to maintain our authenticity without compromising who we are.

Another strategy for staying sharp is to think ahead—always aim to be at least two steps ahead of what's happening in the society you live in. Many people in Western society tend to focus only on today and barely think about tomorrow, let alone weeks, months, or years ahead. This short-sightedness is often why they aren't successful, and they end up blaming outside forces instead of taking responsibility for their own mindset.

Thinking ahead allows you to prepare your life with a sense of order and vision, bringing more certainty to your future. Those who don't plan ahead often get left behind, with no clear direction in life. It's important to avoid surrounding yourself with people who only live for the moment, as they can keep you stuck in a stagnant mindset. Instead, spend time with people who are innovative and have realistic ideas that inspire you to think at a higher level.

It's also helpful to study philosophers, from modern-day thinkers to ancient ones, as they offer unorthodox knowledge that can enhance your ability to think bigger, broader, and wiser. Remember, every action you take in life stems from a thought process. If you ever wonder why you do what you do—whether your actions are positive or negative—take a moment to examine your current mindset. That's where you'll find the answers.

To think efficiently, it's crucial to consistently feed your brain with knowledge. Think of your brain like your body—it needs nourishment. If you starve your mind of knowledge, you'll be less likely to think for yourself, making it difficult to make decisions. This can turn you into a liability to yourself and others. So, it's important to exercise your mind regularly to keep it sharp.

CHAPTER 4

EDUCATING YOURSELF IN BABYLON

Another important aspect of surviving in Babylon is educating yourself. While this might sound simple, many people in the Western world don't pursue education beyond what they've learned in academic institutions. Academic education has its benefits, but it also has its limits. The benefits lie in its usefulness within academic and professional environments, where specific knowledge is needed to perform job roles you've trained for. However, when it comes to navigating real-life situations outside these institutions, academic knowledge may not always be relevant, as it's often not designed to apply beyond the workplace.

This is why many people in the Western world have limited thinking—they only know what they've been taught through the traditional academic system, like school, college, and university, or what they hear on the news. To get ahead in Babylon, you need to engage in revolutionary education, which can bring about a complete change in how you think and operate in society. Revolutionary education is the highest form of learning because it has no limits on where it can take you in life. It can change your perspective on life, improve your communication skills, enhance the quality of your thinking, and offer knowledge beyond what the academic system provides.

There are many avenues for educating yourself, whether it's politics, history, financial literacy, philosophy, or other subjects. For example, if you come from a family that lacks financial literacy, you might want to start studying how to manage money. We live in a society where many people are wasteful with their money. Financial literacy isn't taught in schools, and many modern parents don't take the time to teach their children how to manage money. So, how can the newer generation learn to manage and invest their money wisely if they're not being taught?

This lack of financial literacy explains why Western society is economically poor with little to show for it. People often spend their hard-earned money on material things that offer no real value or benefit. In a Babylonian society that doesn't promote financial literacy, it's crucial to educate yourself on how to use money effectively so that money works for you, rather than you working just for money.

An important part of surviving in Babylon is educating yourself on how to live. With the rise in stress caused by inflation and the increasing cost of living, the average person is under immense pressure. As a result, many people are stuck in survival mode, focusing only on day-to-day existence with no long-term vision for their lives. This mindset often leads to a lack of regard for others, and sometimes even for their own well-being. People may neglect their diet, mental health, and even personal hygiene because they've lost hope or simply don't know how to live beyond just surviving. This mentality can often be passed down from families who have lived the same way, never learning how to truly live.

It's crucial to educate yourself about the foods that will nourish your body rather than harm it. Learn how the government works, especially if you have young children in school. Understand how the school system operates, what the curriculum is, and what your children are actually learning. This knowledge helps you understand how your children's minds are being shaped by their education.

It's also important to educate yourself about the types of people in society, to understand why they behave the way they do and what might be driving their actions. By learning about the society you live in, you can equip yourself with the right knowledge and tools to better navigate the challenges you face.

Educate yourself on how to live beyond survival mode, and explore different ways to live in a society that often tries to dictate a one-size-fits-all lifestyle. Learn how to empower your character and strengthen it to a higher level. Educate yourself on spiritual awareness and how it affects your daily energy and mindset. Understand how your actions impact others, and take the time to study the extent of that impact so you can better manage your relationships and interactions.

If you aim to build generational wealth for your family, consider educating yourself on how to start and run a business. Learn about marketing, understand your target audience, and study successful businesspeople to see what strategies they used. Apply some of those strategies to your own journey toward success.

Consistently updating your knowledge and educating yourself is crucial for personal growth. It allows you to create new ideas that can revolutionise how we live, eat, think, and move our society forward. For society to progress, we must embrace growth through revolutionary education.

We live in a society that is very reactive, and this impulsive, childlike response often hinders personal development. Reacting without thinking often leads to poor decisions and can have a negative impact on your life. It's important to learn the difference between reacting to a situation and responding to it thoughtfully. We must educate ourselves on how to make positive changes in our lives, how to bring about long-term solutions, and how to solve problems so we're not stuck repeating the same mistakes.

Final Thoughts

The conclusion we have come to is education is key to

survive and thrive in Babylon, without education one cannot truly thrive as your lack of knowledge will keep you in a limited state of being which will hinder you from reaching your maximum potential. Bear in mind when I say education is important I am not talking about school or academic education even though those forms of education are still forms of knowledge but I am talking about further education outside of the academic realm, which I have already referred to revolutionary education which is the highest form of education anyone can have because it has no limits and it will also unlock your full potential to succeed to greater heights in life.

CHAPTER 5

YOUR SURROUNDINGS OF PEOPLE IN BABYLON

Many of us have people we surround ourselves with, whether they're good or bad for us. In this chapter, we'll explore how the people we engage with affect our lives and why having the right people around you is crucial for maximising your success. As the old saying goes, "If you want to know who someone is, just look at the people they surround themselves with." This is often a reflection of who they are and their state of being at that time in their life. The people you choose to have around you can greatly influence how far you'll go in life.

It's important to be critical of your surroundings and, from time to time, reassess the people in your life. This helps ensure you're getting the best from those around you. You may need to decide whether to keep certain people in your life or replace them with others who are more beneficial to your well-being.

Here are some questions to consider about your social circle:

Q1. Are the people around you a liability or an asset?

This question is crucial for assessing whether your circle is helping or hindering you. In Babylon's society, we aren't usually taught to evaluate the people around us. Many of us surround ourselves with people who don't benefit us at all, and then we wonder why we're not progressing in life. Some of us have friends who just gossip or live chaotic lives, yet we continue to associate with them. This is quite irrational when you think about it.

Sometimes, we don't realise that certain people in our lives are liabilities because we haven't learned to critically analyse them for who they really are. In today's world, it's important to be careful about who we allow into our lives. If we don't, we risk stagnation—growing older without progressing or developing our character. Living like this can lead to internal frustration, especially when you see time passing by with little to no progress in your life. Use this question as a tool to reflect and get the most out of your relationships.

Q2. Are the people around you helping you grow?

This question encourages you to consider whether your circle is contributing to your personal growth. It's vital to have people around who support your growth, as humanity must evolve with new ideas to advance society and the world. If your current circle isn't helping you grow, it might be time to reassess and consider seeking out new connections that can support your development.

Often, we keep people in our lives out of familiarity, which is understandable, but growth often requires stepping out of our comfort zones. If you want to bring positive change to your life, it's essential to ask whether your current circle is helping you grow. This reflection can help you understand the impact your relationships are having on your life.

Q3. Are the people around you supportive of your ideas?

Take a moment to consider whether the people around you support your innovative ideas, or do they tend to shut them down? While it's important to be realistic, if your ideas are constantly being dismissed, it might be time to reassess your circle. Some people might not believe in your ability to execute your ideas for various reasons, but it's crucial to surround yourself with those who either share your vision or encourage you to bring your ideas to life. Being around people who don't believe in you can be very damaging, as they may stifle your potential growth and success. Over time, this can lead to resentment, which isn't a healthy way to live. It's important to ask this question to evaluate who in your circle is genuinely supportive of your ideas and who isn't, so you can replace those who aren't with people who will help you achieve your goals.

Q4. Do the people around you have your best interests at heart?

This is a crucial question to ask yourself when it comes to your interests. You need to check whether the people around you genuinely want to see your interests move in the right direction. Many people don't realise that some of their friends or acquaintances never had their best interests at heart until they start making progress in life. Only then do they see the true colours of those around them, which can be disappointing and hurtful.

For example, imagine you've been friends with someone for years, and suddenly, as soon as you start making progress in your life, you notice a change in how they treat you. You would expect them to be supportive and have your best interests at heart, but that's not always the case. The mistake here is assuming that your circle cares about your interests without actually assessing who truly does. It's your responsibility to evaluate your surroundings and ensure you have the right people around you.

Q5. Do the people around you motivate you in any way?

Motivation plays a huge role in your life, whether you realise it or not. Without it, you'll struggle to get things done. That's why it's so important to surround yourself with motivated people who are driven to move forward in life. So, ask yourself: do the people around you motivate you in any way? If the answer is no, it might be time to consider finding a new group of people who share the same motivational values as you. It makes sense when you think about it. You'd be surprised how many people are surrounded by others who don't motivate them at all. Being around people who inspire you to make the most of life gives you that extra drive to push yourself. So, always make sure to keep company with people who bring out the best in you.

Q6. Have you been able to learn anything from them?

Learning is a fundamental part of life. It's how we grow, develop, and find better ways to do things. When you're with friends, family, or associates, ask yourself if you're learning anything from them. Being around people you can learn from can help you in many areas of your life—from solving problems to handling personal situations or even considering a new direction in life. The right people can teach you valuable lessons, including mistakes they've made, to help you avoid similar pitfalls and thrive more quickly on your own journey.

It's wise to keep knowledgeable people around you, as they help keep your mind sharp and engaged. Feeding your brain with knowledge is just as important as feeding your body with food. If you starve your mind of knowledge, you become an easy target for manipulation due to your lack of understanding. So, always surround yourself with people who are willing to learn and share their knowledge.

Stay away from those who lack a desire to learn, as they'll only hold you back mentally and keep you in a state of intellectual stagnation. Being stuck in this state prevents you from engaging in meaningful conversations and growing as a person. If everyone were intellectually stagnant, no one would learn from each other, and society would never progress. So, if you're not learning from the people around you, it's time to adopt a new approach—surround yourself with people who stimulate your mind and start distancing yourself from those who serve no purpose in your growth.

Q7. What type of impact have your surroundings had on you?

This is where we need to get really honest with ourselves and assess the impact our surroundings have on our lives. Taking the time to evaluate this is a good habit—it helps us decide whether we should keep the same people around us or find new ones for the sake of our well-being. In a society like ours, it's common to see people surrounded by others who have a negative impact on them, affecting them mentally, spiritually, morally, and even physically. It's as if toxic people attract other toxic people, creating a cycle of negativity.

It's crucial to assess your circle to ensure they're having a positive impact on your life. The influence people have on you can either help you become a better person or break you down into pieces, sometimes beyond repair. Sadly, many people in society have been so badly affected by their surroundings that they've become liabilities to themselves and others.

When considering the impact someone has on you, think about the following:
- How is your mind being affected?
- How does this impact make you feel about yourself?
- How does it affect you spiritually?
- How might this impact affect you in the long term?
- Is the impact positive or negative?
- Does it motivate or demotivate you?

In conclusion, we need to take the impact our surroundings have on us very seriously. The influence others have on our well-being can greatly affect how we live our lives day-to-day and shape our future.\

Q8. Do the people around you understand you as an individual?

Understanding is key to building healthy relationships. Without it, frustration and confusion often follow. It's important to have people in your life who truly understand you—your character, your vision, and the direction you're heading. When those around you understand you, it creates a healthy dynamic where you can enjoy and appreciate their presence for what they bring to your life. On the other hand, surrounding yourself with people who don't understand you can lead to strained, unnatural relationships that won't flourish.

Relationships should be organic, authentic, and free-flowing, creating a safe space where you can express yourself without worrying about being misunderstood. Unfortunately, many people find themselves in circles where they feel the need to hold back key parts of their character or knowledge because they know their surroundings may not fully grasp or appreciate them. This dynamic creates a false sense of connection, where you might feel the need to dumb yourself down or act out of character just to fit in.

You don't want to be in a situation where you're trying too hard to be someone you're not or suppressing your true self, as this will only drain your energy and pull you away from who you really are. When you're not around the right people who understand you, you may find yourself getting lost in a character that's completely opposite to who you are, leading to confusion and conflict within your identity.

In conclusion, the wrong people around you aren't necessarily bad people; they just aren't on the same level of understanding as you at this point in time. This means you need to seek out people who share your values and have a similar level of understanding about life.

Q9. - Do the people around you drain your energy or energise you?

Energy is a powerful force, and it's important to understand its influence on us and those around us. Whether we realise it or not, our surroundings have an impact on our energy levels, so it's crucial to assess whether the people in our lives are draining or energising us. Have you ever visited someone and noticed that, after parting ways, you feel completely drained? Perhaps you left your house feeling energised, but by the time you return, your energy has significantly dropped. If this happens regularly with a particular friend, it might be time to re-evaluate that relationship and consider distancing yourself for the sake of your own well-being.

It's important to surround yourself with people who bring joy and positive energy into your life—people who can bring out the best in you and speak life into you. This kind of interaction is incredibly healthy for your mind, body, and spirit.

The conclusion we can draw is that if the people around you are draining your energy, it's essential to retreat by distancing yourself from them. This could mean stepping back from a family member, friends you've grown up with, or any other familiar faces in your life. Sometimes, it's necessary to move on and spend time alone until you find new, healthier connections that uplift and energise your spirit.

Q10. Are you the smartest person in your circle?

Take a moment to look at your current surroundings and ask yourself if you're the smartest person in your circle. If the answer is yes, you might initially think that's a good thing—you may feel confident because you have more knowledge than those around you. While being the smartest in your group can be beneficial to others, as they can learn a lot from you, it's important to consider what you're learning from them.

For knowledge to be truly effective, it needs to flow in both directions. If you and your circle are sharing knowledge with each other, it creates an atmosphere of continuous learning that benefits everyone. However, if you're the smartest person in your group, the knowledge only flows one way—from you to them—with nothing flowing back to you. This can leave you in a position where you're not growing or learning from others.

It's important to surround yourself with people who may know more than you do in certain areas, as this allows you to learn from them and continue progressing in your journey through life.

CHAPTER 6

————

HOW TO SURVIVE IN A WESTERN SOCIETY IN BABYLON

Surviving in Western society is becoming more challenging every day. You can see it in the way people live and interact with each other—more people are begging on the streets, mental health issues are on the rise, suicide rates are climbing, stress levels are increasing due to the cost of living, and there's a growing sense of isolation. Families are becoming fractured, and problems like depression, alcohol, and drug abuse are more common than ever. These issues are causing many people to lose hope and motivation to change their situations, and they end up surrounding themselves with people who are more of a burden than a help, simply because it's easier to stay comfortable in their conditions.

In times like these, it's crucial to take action and avoid getting trapped in the cycles of Babylon. Let's explore some healthy ways to improve our living conditions and achieve what we want in life.

#1 - Speaking Life into Yourself

Speak life into yourself through your mind, body, and spirit. Even when your current situation makes you feel otherwise, it's important to speak positivity into existence. Remember, what you feel and what you speak are two different things. Just because you're feeling down doesn't mean you can't speak something positive into your life at that moment.

If you're going through difficult times, tell yourself that you'll be okay and that you'll rise above the challenge. But don't stop there—follow it up with a plan of action to change your situation. You can't just sit around hoping for your life to improve; you need to speak what you want into existence and then put in the work to achieve it. Tell yourself that you will accomplish even the most challenging goals, even if others say you can't, even if they don't believe in you, and even if part of you has doubts. Push those doubts aside, test yourself, and see what you can achieve.

Speaking life into yourself can ignite a relentless drive within you, one that may be difficult to explain to others. It can energise your mind and body with a powerful force that propels you forward in whatever you're trying to accomplish. In a society filled with negativity, speaking life into yourself is a powerful tool to keep positive energy flowing through your mind and body. It's also a crucial survival tool in Babylon, helping you stay motivated, energised, and driven to do what you need to do every day. And remember, it's equally important to surround yourself with people who speak life into you as well.

#2 - Self-Motivation

Some people might wonder what self-motivation means. Well, the term itself is quite straightforward—it means being motivated by yourself. You might argue that people need support in life, and that's true, especially for those who have disabilities or health issues and can't take care of themselves. But here, we're talking about able-bodied individuals who can do things for themselves.

In today's Western society, where everyone is often looking out for themselves, you might not always get the support you need. That's why it's important to start relying more on yourself to get things done. It's time to develop the habit of being self-motivated because you won't always have others around to push you or bring out the best in you.

Being self-motivated requires a lot of inner strength. Your mind needs to be clear and focused because it's not an easy thing to do. Many people in Western society aren't naturally self-motivated because they've been spoiled—whether by overprotective parents or by the material things they have, like the latest phone, expensive gaming consoles, clothes, or a sense of entitlement. Being spoiled doesn't foster self-motivation; if anything, it can make you lazy and diminish your drive to do things for yourself. That's why facing challenges and experiencing a bit of struggle can help build character.

What often happens to people who've had support for a long time is that when it suddenly disappears, they don't know what to do with themselves. They become weak and struggle to stand on their own two feet, unable to navigate life using their own internal resources. By internal resources, I mean your mind, your inner strength, your knowledge, or even the skills you've developed that can help you move forward in life.

It's important not to become too dependent on others—not because you're too proud to ask for help, but because people won't always be available to support you. Everyone has their own problems and struggles, and sometimes they might not have the capacity to help you, leaving you to manage on your own.

Self-motivation can be a heavy burden to carry because you're often relying on yourself to get things done, which can be exhausting. So, it's important to take time to rest when you're pushing yourself to the limit. While self-motivation is a powerful tool, it can also have its downsides and put a strain on your mental, spiritual, and physical health. It's essential to use self-motivation in moderation and not overdo it, as it can be both a builder and a destroyer.

Let's explore some of the positives and negatives of self-motivation.

Positives of Self-Motivation

- Builds strength of character
- Increases confidence
- Creates a no-excuse attitude
- Encourages self-accountability
- Promotes self-reliance
- Enhances thinking capacity
- Fosters self-empowerment

Negatives of Self-Motivation

- Risk of burnout
- Increased stress
- Feeling overwhelmed
- Potential for self-neglect
- Can lead to depression
- Struggle to be content with success

Self-motivation is a powerful tool, but it must be used with balance, moderation, and understanding. Overusing it can lead to problems, so it's important not to rely on it too heavily.

#3 - Freedom

Freedom is something many of us in Western society haven't truly experienced. What do I mean by this? Let's dive a bit deeper. Think about your life from childhood to adulthood. You were told what to do by your parents, at nursery, at school, and even at work. Notice the pattern? Nursery, school, and work are all controlled environments where you're expected to conform to their rules and ways of thinking. None of these places teach you to think for yourself; instead, you're conditioned to follow a way of thinking that isn't your own.

Ask yourself, when have you ever truly had the freedom to think for yourself? When have you had the freedom to live life on your own terms? It's important to seek freedom, starting with yourself. Begin by freeing your mind from any chains that are keeping you stuck in the same mindset you've been in for some time. Free yourself from any grudges you're holding onto from people who may have hurt you in the past. I know it's hard to let go of hurt and pain, but holding onto that negativity won't serve you well in the long term.

Ask yourself, what purpose does holding onto a grudge serve? How will it help you now and in the future? What good comes from clinging to pain? Is the grudge you're holding hurting you more than the person you're begrudging? These are important questions to ask because they help you look at your life on a deeper level. Holding grudges will only make you bitter, cloud your vision, and negatively impact how you see people and life. Depending on how deep the grudge is, it can even affect your physical health. It's vital to free yourself from these grudges so you can move forward more efficiently on your journey and create a sense of freedom within yourself—freeing your mind, body, and spirit from the burdens you carry.

Free your mind from ignorance by engaging in revolutionary education that transforms your thinking and helps break through the mental stagnation that keeps your mind limited. Free yourself from any problems weighing down your spirit and draining your energy day by day. While life will always throw challenges your way—that's just part of the journey—you can choose to approach life more holistically to get the results you need to move forward.

Let's explore ways to free ourselves from our burdens and solve our problems more effectively.

Step 1: Acknowledge that you have a problem.

Acknowledging that you have a problem is the first step towards solving it. It shows you're ready to start dealing with the issue and that you're aware something needs to be addressed.

Step 2: Talk about the problem

Talking about the problem helps you come to terms with what you're going through. By discussing it, you make the problem more real and start to process your feelings about it.

Step 3: Assess how your problem has affected you

Assessing how your problem has impacted your life is a crucial part of the process. It helps you understand the extent of the damage, whether it's mental, emotional, or spiritual. This step removes the illusion that everything is fine when, in reality, it might not be.

Step 4: Come up with a solution to tackle the issue

In this step, you create a plan to solve your problem. There's no one-size-fits-all approach—just choose a solution that works best for you. Make sure your solution doesn't create new problems, as that would only delay resolving the issue.

Believe it or not, many people don't even make it past the first step of acknowledging they have a problem. This is what we call denial. Admitting you have a problem means you have to face it, and that's something many people shy away from. In a society like ours, which can be quite toxic, you might notice that people often try to take shortcuts when dealing with issues. They might sweep their problems under the carpet, distract themselves with irrelevant things, or even turn to substance abuse or other forms of escapism to avoid facing the truth.

Some people go as far as convincing themselves that they don't have a problem at all, which is a dangerous form of denial. Ignoring a problem doesn't make it go away; it just prolongs the inevitable. The longer you put off dealing with an issue, the harder it becomes to resolve because life keeps throwing more challenges your way. This can lead to a situation where problems pile up on top of one another, making it even more difficult to address the root cause.

When the root of a problem isn't dealt with, it tends to grow, giving rise to more issues that can overshadow the original problem. This is why it's so important to tackle problems head-on; otherwise, they can cause long-term damage to your well-being, potentially leaving you in a state where you're beyond repair. Once you reach this point, no one can help you, and you become a liability not only to yourself but also to those around you. This leads to a cycle of chaos, bringing more problems into your life and affecting others too.

The key takeaway here is that running away from your problems won't lead to the freedom you're seeking. Instead, it creates a prison within yourself, which eventually manifests in your external life as well. To truly live a life of freedom, you must free yourself from all forms of internal bondage. Without freeing yourself from within, you'll remain trapped in a cycle of internal struggle.

#4 - Mental Prison

Another key aspect of being truly free is escaping your own mental prison. A mental prison is made up of repetitive thoughts that loop endlessly in your mind, trapping you in a cycle that can be hard to break, especially if these thoughts are deeply rooted in your psyche.

To free yourself, strive to be a freethinking individual who isn't confined to one way of thinking. Diversifying your mind involves exposing it to new knowledge regularly. If you deprive your mind of knowledge, you keep it locked in a state of mental confinement. Being open to learning new things and gaining insights from others can broaden your thinking as well.

It's also important to consider the people around you. If your circle isn't elevating their minds—whether due to laziness or refusal to seek out new information—they're likely to stagnate mentally. If you consistently keep such people around, you risk being stuck in the same mindset.

Many of us end up in a mental prison because of the illusions we hold onto. We might not even realise we're living in an illusionary world. Social media plays a huge role in this, as it influences many people's views on life. In an isolated society where much of life is lived online, it's easy to mistake what you see on social media as the truth, especially when people are saying anything to gain clout, clicks, and views. Unfortunately, today's generation is often shaped by the content they consume on the internet.

If you constantly expose yourself to negative content online, it can create a mental prison of illusions. For example, if you're on social media and see everyone posting pictures and videos of how great their lives seem, while your life isn't going well, you might start believing that everyone else is thriving. This could lead you to feel like a failure, even though the reality of others' lives might be just as challenging as yours, if not worse. This is an illusionary mental prison that keeps you from making real progress in your own life.

Some people watch reality TV shows and secretly fantasise about living the lavish lifestyles of the celebrities they see on screen. They start comparing their own lives to these celebrities and end up telling themselves they're not good enough because they don't have the same lifestyle. This creates another illusion in their mind, forming a mental prison they become trapped in.

Others might convince themselves that they're nobody unless they own certain material things, like expensive clothes, shoes, or jewellery. This is another form of mental programming that society often pushes on people. There's also the belief that to gain acknowledgement or respect, you must look wealthy—dressing in high-end brands and flaunting luxury items. But in reality, you don't need any of those things to be respected or valued, even if society tries to tell you otherwise.

The mind is incredibly powerful but also fragile, so it's crucial to be mindful of the thoughts you allow to take root, especially negative ones that can create a mental prison.

The media is another dangerous tool that can place illusions in people's minds, often trapping them in mental prisons. The way information is presented can be very persuasive. For instance, the news often focuses on negative events, showing all the bad things happening in the world while rarely highlighting the positive. Consuming too much of this kind of news can make you believe that nothing good ever happens, even though there are many people doing positive things in their communities that don't get covered. This tactic keeps you in a state of fear, anxiety, and depression, giving you a skewed, negative view of the world.

It's crucial to free ourselves from our mental prisons, as they can stop us from thinking clearly and effectively in our daily lives. The best way to do this is by removing the limits we place on our minds, living more in reality, and letting go of the illusions that hold us back. Let's quickly look at how we can eliminate these illusions from our minds:

- Recognise that your mind is caught in an illusion.
- Acknowledge where this mental illusion came from.
- Understand that only you have the power to create and destroy your own illusions.

- Start seeing things for what they really are.
- Begin living your life based on reality.

The aim here is to realise that you are both the creator and the destroyer of your own illusions. Only you can free yourself from them by choosing to live in reality and truth, as these are the remedies that will cure the illusions in your mind.

#5 - Celebrating Western Holidays

One of the key ways to survive in Babylon is to stay focused and avoid distractions that don't add value to your life. I understand that many people celebrate Western holidays because it's what they've known since childhood, and these celebrations are heavily promoted in schools and across society. Let's take a look at some of the main holidays that most people acknowledge each year:

- Valentine's Day
- Easter
- Christmas

When you celebrate these holidays, there's a common pattern: you end up spending money that could be better spent on things with long-term value. Ask yourself, if you didn't spend money on these holidays, what else could you invest in? Think about those times when you've said you can't afford something throughout the year. Now, consider how much you spend annually on Valentine's Day, Easter, and Christmas. Could it be that if you didn't indulge in these celebrations, you might have had the money to buy some of the things you said you couldn't afford? It's worth reflecting on that.

When you celebrate these holidays, ask yourself: what do they mean to you? What significance do they hold in your life? What benefit do you gain from participating in them? Is spending money on these holidays a liability or an asset to your life?

Think about the effort and stress you go through to celebrate these holidays throughout the year. Consider the amount of mental energy you spend worrying about how many Easter eggs to buy, whether it's for your kids, nieces, or nephews. Think about the unnecessary pressure you put on yourself to celebrate Valentine's Day, and the stress of rushing around before Christmas to buy expensive presents, standing in long queues because everyone else is doing the same. All that energy spent, and for what? A celebration? Are these Western holidays really worth the stress and money you pour into them?

You might be wondering why these questions are being raised. The reason is simple: we are living in crucial times, and the cost of living keeps rising. For your own survival, it's important to be mindful of your finances and how you spend your money. If you're serious about securing a stable future for yourself and your family, or if you're focused on building wealth and leaving a legacy for future generations, you might want to reconsider participating in these Western celebrations.

These holidays are often just distractions that can drain your finances and add unnecessary stress to your life. I'm not saying you can't celebrate these holidays, but if you're focused on building wealth and aiming for a more stress-free lifestyle, stepping back from these celebrations could help you achieve that goal. This isn't about criticising those who enjoy these holidays; it's about speaking to those who are serious about their present and future survival in Babylon, and who want to free themselves from the unnecessary worries of celebrating holidays that may hold little real significance for them.

#6 - Healing

Another essential tool for surviving and thriving in Babylon is healing. When we look around at the society we live in, it's clear that many people are walking around deeply damaged. What's even more concerning is that a lot of these people don't even realise they're in desperate need of healing. We're living in a time where dysfunctional behaviour has become the norm, and whether we realise it or not, we're seeing the damaged leading the damaged.

Many people are so traumatised by their experiences that they unknowingly spread their emotional pain to others, like a contagious disease. The majority of those who are damaged manage to wear a mask in public, concealing their hurt, pain, and trauma. On the surface, they might seem fine, but spend enough time around them, and you'll start to see the cracks, revealing their deep emotional scars.

What's troubling is that if you try to confront some people about their dysfunctions, they might become defensive or even hostile. They might insist there's nothing wrong with them and reject the idea of needing any form of help. This is not a healthy way to live and is incredibly harmful to your well-being.

In a society that's becoming more challenging by the day, and under a government that seems to neglect the people it's supposed to care for, you need to be highly functional to survive and thrive. You can't do that if you're damaged beyond repair. To begin the healing process, you must start by asking yourself some important questions:

- Is there anyone in your life you're holding a grudge against?
- If yes, how long have you been holding onto this grudge?
- What's stopping you from letting go of this grudge?
- What purpose does holding onto this grudge serve?
- How has this grudge impacted your life?
- When will you start the process of letting go?
- Are there any past pains or traumas that still affect you today?
- How have these past pains and traumas affected you over

the years?

• Do you know how to start the healing process within yourself?

The questions above are crucial because they help you reflect on and acknowledge the issues that have been affecting you for years. They guide you towards starting the healing process, which begins with admitting that you're a damaged individual in need of repair. If you can't admit that you need healing, you'll remain stuck in a state of dysfunction, which isn't going to help you survive in Babylon.

We live in a society built on chaos, dysfunction, and disorder. The government thrives on our disarray, so to take back control, we need to get ourselves in order by recognising our own dysfunctions and working to become better-functioning human beings through healing. One key step in this process is forgiving those who have hurt us in the past. I understand this can be difficult, but letting go of past pain can lighten your emotional load. Forgiving doesn't mean forgetting or rekindling friendships with those who hurt you; it simply means releasing the bitterness that will otherwise eat away at you from within.

Holding onto bitterness will eventually destroy you, affecting your relationships with family, friends, and everyone in your life. As you grow older, this bitterness can consume you more and more, leaving you isolated and alone. Over time, you may find that you've lost many connections because of the grudges and past pains you never addressed.

Think of your past pains and traumas like a child that needs care, attention, and nurturing. To properly heal and move forward, you need to "feed" these dysfunctions with the following five healing principles:

(i) Acknowledgment

Acknowledging that you are carrying past traumas and that these are negatively impacting your life is the first step towards healing. It's about recognising that these dysfunctions need to be addressed.

(ii) Forgiveness

Forgiveness is what you need to offer to your past or present traumas, bitterness, and grudges. To move on from what someone has done to you, whether in the past or present, you need to forgive them, no matter how much it hurts. Forgiving isn't just about the other person; it's about your own peace of mind and sanity. It's about freeing yourself from the heavy burden you've been carrying for so long.

(iii) Love

To let go of any anger, hate, or grudges in your heart, the best way to combat these feelings is with love. This means having enough love for yourself not to burden your heart with toxic emotions. Love yourself enough to live a life free from hate, grudges, and bitterness, which only lead to dysfunctional behaviour. The key message here is to protect your heart with love, not hate.

(iv) Care

To heal your traumas, you need to care for them. This means addressing each one directly and with intention. Don't ignore your traumas; if you do, they'll grow unchecked within you, eventually leading to an emotional explosion. By caring for your wounded traumas, you'll find that you can function much better in life. Attending to your traumas helps you operate in a more balanced and wholesome way.

(v) Peace

To live with the traumas that linger inside, you must eventually make peace with them and accept that they are now part of who you are. The more you resist, the more you'll be at war with yourself, creating a never-ending struggle. Traumatic scars don't simply disappear; they stay with you forever. Your task is to learn how to live with them.

Think of it like sharing a house with someone. For you both to live together successfully, you need to respect each other's space and coexist peacefully. Now, consider your trauma as that person—it's inside you and isn't going away. Many people in Western society make the mistake of constantly fighting with themselves instead of simply making peace with their past experiences. Living peacefully within yourself allows you to function better and live more efficiently.

If you're holding onto grudges, bitterness, or traumas that are holding you back, the best approach is to make peace with those inner wounds and with anyone who may have wronged you. But remember, before you can make peace with others, you must first make peace with yourself.

#7 - Stability

To survive in Babylon, one of the key tools you need is stability. When people think of stability, they often focus on finances, having a big house, a nice car, and expensive clothes. This is the narrative society pushes as the definition of being stable. But the kind of stability I'm talking about is being stable within yourself. For example, to function efficiently, it's crucial to be stable mentally, emotionally, spiritually, and even physically. If you lack stability in any of these areas, you'll find yourself living in chaos and dysfunction, no matter your financial status—whether you're wealthy, rich, or poor. Let's explore the different levels of stability.

(i) Mental Stability

To operate effectively, your mental health needs to have a certain level of balance. If your mental health isn't stable, you won't be able to function at your best. It's important to check in on your mental health regularly to understand where you stand mentally. Positive thinking plays a huge role in this—when faced with a problem, instead of falling into a victim mindset with thoughts like "why me?" or "poor me," the healthy approach is to think of a solution to address the problem without delaying it.

Thinking about your future is also a sign of good mental health because it shows that you believe you have a future worth planning for. This mindset encourages you to do everything within your power to ensure you experience that future, which is a positive way to think and live. Being mentally stable means having a positive outlook on life, maintaining high self-esteem, and believing in yourself and your abilities.

(ii) Emotional Stability

Emotional stability is crucial, especially in today's society, where so many people struggle to control their emotions, leading to chaos for themselves and others. Being emotionally stable means having the ability to respond thoughtfully to life's challenges rather than reacting impulsively. It involves managing and controlling your emotions so that you can make rational decisions without letting your feelings cloud your judgement.

Emotional stability also means not acting on your emotions too quickly but taking a moment to think before you react. If you find yourself frequently reacting impulsively, it might be time to take a closer look at yourself and ask some important questions:

- Why do I always react so quickly?
- Why am I so easily triggered by even the smallest things?
- When did I start behaving this way?
- Where did I learn this reactionary behaviour?
- Who influenced me to act this way?
- Is there a better way to handle my emotions?

Emotional stability is an essential tool for surviving in Babylon. Without it, life can become chaotic, disordered, and dysfunctional, leading to torment, self-torture, misery, and constant discomfort. The key takeaway here is that if you or those around you notice any signs of emotional instability, it's a clear indication that you need to take steps to improve your emotional well-being.

(iii) Spiritual Stability

Being spiritually stable is another crucial tool for surviving in Babylon. You might wonder how to maintain spiritual stability in times like these, filled with chaos, noise, violence, unrest, injustice, and distractions. To understand this, consider that there is a spiritual version of you and a physical version, and both are directly connected. Whatever you experience and feel on a physical level will impact your spirit and its ability to stay balanced.

For example, if your life is filled with chaos, dysfunction, and discomfort, your spirit will absorb the energy from these experiences, leading to spiritual fatigue. Just as your body tires physically, your spirit can also become weary. Whatever you feed your spirit, it will react to—if you constantly feed it negativity, your spirit will operate at a low vibration. Others around you might sense this low energy and may even distance themselves because your low vibration could drain their spiritual energy.

If you find that your spirit is operating at a low vibration, it's a sign of spiritual imbalance. In such cases, it's essential to restore balance to your spirit, which will help keep you motivated and driven. Here are some basic ways to uplift your spirit in times of spiritual distress:

- **Speak Positivity into Yourself**

Speaking positivity into yourself helps to generate a flow of positive energy within your mind and body. However, simply speaking positive words isn't enough—they need to be backed by action. Words alone won't make a difference, but they can ignite the motivation you need to start your journey toward success.

- **Surround Yourself with Positive People**

Never underestimate the power of being around positive people who keep your spirit uplifted. These are the kinds of people you need in your life to maintain a positive attitude, which in turn helps you stay mentally strong throughout your journey, no matter what circumstances you face.

- **Keep Your Future Goals at the Forefront of Your Mind**

Keeping your future goals consistently at the forefront of your mind can be a powerful motivator. Have you ever envisioned your future and felt a spark of excitement, like a fire lighting up inside you? That's the feeling you need to nurture and maintain to create a relentless drive that propels you forward. Always keep your goals in focus, and steer clear of things or people that might distract you from your goal-oriented mindset.

- **Engage in Activities That Empower You.**

Taking part in activities that empower you is vital for your spiritual stability. For example, if you're healing from past traumas, joining a healing group where you can share with others on a similar journey can be incredibly supportive.

Engaging in activities that make you feel good about yourself is key to uplifting your spirit. When your spirit is constantly uplifted, it feeds off the positive energy you create through these empowering activities, helping you maintain spiritual stability.

• **Acknowledge the Positive Aspects of Your Character**

Recognising the positive aspects of your character is essential for maintaining spiritual balance. If you ever find yourself questioning your abilities, it's important to take a moment to reflect on the good qualities you possess. This self-assessment can remind you of the positive traits that bring balance to your spirit, helping to restore a sense of inner harmony.

• **Reflect on How Far You've Come in Life**

When you're doubting yourself, one of the best things you can do is reflect on how far you've come. It's easy to get caught up in negative thoughts, believing you haven't achieved enough, but often you've accomplished more than you realise. Downplaying your achievements can weigh down your spirit and hinder your motivation. Remembering your progress helps raise your spirit's vibration, allowing you to maintain a steady flow of growth and progress in your life.

• **Reflect on the Positive Impact You've Had on Others**

One way to keep your spiritual balance in check is by reflecting on the positive impact you've had on the lives of others, whether it's friends, family, or colleagues. When you think about the good you've done, you send positive energy to your spirit, which thrives on this uplifting force. Remember the joy and happiness you felt when you saw how your actions positively affected those around you? That's the kind of energy you need to sustain to keep your spirit vibrating at a high frequency.

• **Embrace the Endless Possibilities in Life**

Life is full of endless possibilities, and it's important to approach it with a mindset that there are no limits to what you can achieve. The saying "the sky is the limit" can actually be a form of psychological programming, subtly suggesting that there's a ceiling to how far you can go. But think about it—do the wealthiest, most successful people in the world live by that phrase? The same government that continues to take more from its citizens doesn't believe in limits, which is why the gap between the rich and poor keeps growing. So why would you limit your own potential? Telling yourself that there are limits to what you can achieve doesn't push you to reach your maximum potential. This limited thinking weighs down your spirit, making it harder to maintain spiritual stability. Instead, focus on keeping your spirit high and embracing the endless possibilities life has to offer.

Conclusion

Spiritual stability is crucial for surviving and thriving in Babylon. Without it, life can descend into chaos, causing harm not only to yourself but also to those around you. By maintaining a strong spiritual balance, you create a foundation for a more peaceful and fulfilling life.

#8- Knowing your worth

I am sure many of you have heard this statement before "know your worth" but do we really what it means to know our worth?   In western society what I seem to see is worth is measured in what it is you have in terms material things like having a nice car, wearing expensive clothes, having a big house etc, when you speak to a lot of young people who still live with their parents you normally here them say they are saving up to buy a house, now don't get me wrong we all need somewhere to live and lay and sleep every night don't we? what I am saying is that buying a house seems to be associated with having some sort of status and worth when the reality is the house you are buying is not completely yours until you pay off all your mortgage and also you don't own the land that the house it built on but yet you still worth of the house because this is one of the societal narratives of how worth is measured. If you don't drive a luxurious car or look like you are rich then people seem to think that you are just another average person, whereas in some cases the most wealthiest do not dress flamboyantly neither do they wear expensive jewellery, wear expensive footwear nor to some extent don't even drive expensive cars as they see that as a financial liability, the rich tend to lease cars instead on a 3 year basis instead of actually owning the car as they don't see their worth through such material things.

When it comes to knowing your worth it's not something that cost money, knowing your worth has nothing to do with money or what it is you have, it's a priceless gift from life to yourself, life itself is where the real worth is at, without life itself none of us would be here to enjoy the things we love doing. To understand your worth is to ask these questions:

- What is your character worth?
- How much is your time worth?
- How valuable is your knowledge?
- How much life experience do you have?
- What can people learn from you?
- Are you able to give sound advice to others?
- What type of mindset do you have?
- What skills do you have to offer?
- How much help can you be to yourself and others?

When you measure your worth, try not to think about material possessions or the money you have. The reason I say this is because if you equate your worth to money, you're essentially saying that you can be bought or sold. If you can be bought or sold, it means your worth isn't rare or unique. It means others can use you, then discard you when they're done. But true worth can't be bought, sold, or replicated. Each of us has our own unique value.

Knowing your worth means knowing yourself. If you don't know your worth, you become a slave to someone else's idea of value. You fall victim to someone else's or society's definition of what self-worth is. Look at people who don't know their worth —they often get taken advantage of, used, and thrown away when they're no longer needed. This happens because they lack the knowledge and understanding of their true value.

The Babylon system we live in doesn't teach us how to discover our own self-worth. If it did, people might start questioning the system's values, leading to critical thinking and progressive conversations. These could inspire people to take control of their lives, which isn't something the system encourages. That's why it's crucial to understand the importance of self-worth and to gain knowledge of yourself. This knowledge opens the door to exploring the unique set of values you have to offer yourself and those around you.

The key message here is simple: to survive in Babylon, you must know your worth. It's the foundation for growth, thriving, and succeeding to your fullest potential.

#9 - Be at peace with yourself

To survive and thrive in Babylon, it's crucial to find peace within yourself. Many of us are constantly battling with ourselves, dealing with internal issues like trauma, stress, and anxiety, which create a lot of unrest inside. This inner turmoil, if left unchecked, eventually surfaces and affects our ability to think or act rationally. Many of us don't know how to handle our traumas, nor do we realise the importance of letting go of the emotional baggage we've carried for years. We often believe that running away from ourselves will solve our deep-rooted problems, but in reality, this just adds more complications as new challenges arise. Problems will always come our way, so it's important to face them and accept how they've impacted our wellbeing.

Being at peace with yourself is one of the greatest gifts you can give yourself in your daily life. But you might wonder how to find peace when there's so much noise and chaos in the world around us. When you step outside into the noisy society, the best way to stay peaceful is to be still and let the noise pass through you. Understand that this might disturb your spirit, and you might feel irritable. This irritation is the noise of society passing through your body as you go about your day. In these moments, don't react—just remain silent and let the process happen.

As you go about your day, keep your mind focused on your mission—where you're going and what you want to achieve. Don't let the noise of society distract you, because that noise has nothing to do with you and is beyond your control. Learn to be at peace with the fact that you can't control everything. Don't waste your energy and time complaining about things or people you can't change. When you live without worrying about things beyond your control, life becomes much more peaceful. The inner peace you can achieve at this point is incomparable.

We live in a society consumed by drama, to the point where it has become normal. Families are filled with drama, reality TV shows thrive on it, and social media often showcases videos of people fighting—more drama. Being caught in this cycle is unhealthy for both your mind and spirit. This drama-filled existence keeps us in a toxic state, which is exactly what Babylon wants. The system thrives on chaos and disorder, keeping us from thinking clearly and rationally. It keeps us confused, creating the illusion that peace is boring and that chaos is necessary to enjoy life. People who live peacefully are often seen as dull.

Have you ever been somewhere or visited someone's house where it was so peaceful and quiet that you found yourself bored? Think about it—that was your chance to have a moment of peace and unplug from all the noise and stress in your life, yet you complained. There are people out there who rarely get any time to themselves due to work and family commitments. Over time, this lack of peace and quiet builds up unhealthy levels of stress in their minds and bodies.

To survive and thrive in Babylon, it's important to use the tool of peace to navigate each day effectively. Remember, peace is not a place or a destination; it's a state of mind and a way of life. Let's explore some simple ways to create peace within ourselves.

- **First, accept any trauma within you**
The first step towards healing is accepting that you have trauma. If you don't acknowledge it, you'll always be at war with yourself, causing harm not just to yourself but also to those around you. Accepting your trauma opens the door to understanding how it has impacted your life.

- **Address how it has affected your life**
Once you've accepted your trauma, it's time to explore how it has shaped your thoughts and the decisions you've made. This step involves looking in the mirror and facing some uncomfortable truths about how the trauma has influenced your life. It might be difficult because it's something you've avoided for a long time, but addressing it is crucial for moving towards healing.

- **Begin the healing process**

After addressing the impact of your trauma, it's important to start healing. This is where you work to replace dysfunctional behaviours with healthier ones. Surround yourself with supportive people who can help you on this journey. It's essential to distance yourself from toxic influences during this time, as they can hinder your progress and keep you stuck.

- **Accept that your trauma is part of you now**

One key aspect of healing is accepting that your trauma will always be a part of you. It's not something that will just fade away, and that's okay. Trying to escape it will only lead to an ongoing internal battle. If you can accept that your trauma is now part of your life, you'll find it easier to move forward in the long run.

- **Learn to live with your trauma and find peace with it**

Once you've accepted your trauma, the next step is to learn how to live with it and make peace with it. Don't fight it—trying to get rid of something that's already part of you is a losing battle. Instead, accept it and move on. Many people struggle because they keep fighting or running from their trauma, not realising that making peace with it can bring them the inner calm they seek.

Imagine two people at war with each other. If neither is willing to make peace, the war continues, affecting not only them but also those around them. In the end, the conflict could destroy both of them and have devastating effects on others. The solution is for them to make peace, allowing them to live their lives without consuming themselves with anger and hatred.

In dealing with your trauma, the approach should be the same. Don't fight it—make peace with it, accept it as part of your life, and learn to live with it. Think of trauma as a long-term partner you have to work with for the rest of your life. If you approach it with a mindset of healing, your trauma can become a source of wisdom rather than a burden.

The important takeaway here is that to survive in Babylon, you need to find peace within yourself. Without inner peace, you risk self-destruction, which could ruin your entire life. Peace is the greatest gift you can give yourself as you navigate through life.

#10 - Live Your Life with Purpose

One of the most important things we need to do to survive in Babylon is to live our lives with purpose. Living with purpose gives your life meaning, a reason to get up every day and do what you do. Sadly, in western society, many people wake up each day and just drift through life without any real purpose or meaning. Some people spend their whole lives just coasting along, not really knowing what their purpose is. To live without purpose is, in many ways, a waste of life. Some might disagree and say, "But I've had a lot of fun, travelled to many places, so has my life been a waste?" The question then is: what was your purpose for doing all those things? There's nothing wrong with having fun, visiting new places, or travelling the world, but if you're doing things without purpose, at some point, you have to ask yourself, what is the meaning behind it all? What is the point of getting up every day if there's no purpose behind your actions? Are you just going through the motions for the sake of it?

When we take a look at the society we live in, we have to acknowledge that we're living in a world that often lacks purpose. Most people are just doing things without questioning why, simply following societal trends because they're popular. This is why western society is in decline, and it's only getting worse. A large part of the population doesn't take responsibility for the society they live in. When a significant percentage of people refuse to contribute new ideas or fulfil their daily roles, you can't expect society to make progress; you can only expect it to fall apart, which is what we're seeing now in Babylon.

The government continues to use and exploit the people, and nobody does anything about it. Instead, people remain passive, accepting whatever the government throws at them. The government acts like a bully, and the people are like frightened children who won't stand up for themselves. If you don't stand up to the bully, the bullying will continue until you say enough is enough. Many of us don't realise it's our responsibility to bring about change in the society we live in because we lack self-awareness. Without knowing who you are, you can't know your purpose, and without purpose, life lacks meaning.

In a state of confusion one may ask how do you go about finding your purpose in life? Let us ask some question that will help you to find your purpose:

Who Are You? Asking yourself this question gives you the chance to explore different aspects of your current character. This is the moment to reflect on who you are right now, whether or not you have a clear answer. At some stage, you'll need to answer this question before you can truly embark on your life's purpose. Many people today don't know who they are because they're too focused on external influences, letting others define them instead of discovering their own identity. You need to live by an identity that feels genuine to you, something that aligns with your character. Knowing who you are helps keep you on track with your purpose in life.

What Type of Person Do You Aspire to Be? To pursue your purpose, you need to figure out what kind of person you want to become. This isn't about copying someone else, but about evolving into the best version of yourself. We should always aim to grow as we get older, not remain stagnant. Set high aspirations for yourself, even if others don't see your potential.

What Do You Want to Do with Your Life? Life offers so much. At some point, take time out of your daily routine to figure out what you want from life. Knowing what you want gives you a focus point to help you fulfil your purpose.

What Do You Stand For? To fulfil your purpose, it's crucial to know what you stand for. If you're not sure yet, spend some time getting to know yourself better. If you already have an idea of what you want to represent but lack the confidence to stand by it, your task is to build up your self-confidence and courage. You need to reach a point where you no longer feel the need to hide your true beliefs and values.

What skills do you have? Fulfilling your purpose isn't just about taking action; it also involves having the right skills to drive your purpose forward. Ask yourself what skills you have that can help you take your purpose to the next level. If you don't have any particular skills at the moment, think about what new skills you'd like to learn to improve yourself. Purpose isn't something that works alone; it's connected to other aspects like your identity, who you aspire to be, knowing what you want from life, and understanding what you stand for.

When you embark on your purpose, you need to be aware of what that choice entails. It's not an easy path to walk. People who choose to fulfil their purpose often find themselves walking that journey alone for a long time before they meet others who might join them on their quest for success. Living your purpose isn't a game, and it's not something you need to talk about constantly. Your purpose is a way of life that only you can live because it's uniquely yours. It's something that has been waiting for you your whole life, and now that you've found it, you must unite with it and pursue it relentlessly until you achieve the results you're aiming for.

Pursuing your purpose in Babylon requires you to be militant, disciplined, serious, focused, determined, and relentless, all at the same time. Before you start pursuing your purpose, ask yourself these questions:

How serious are you about your purpose? First, ask yourself how serious you are about completing this journey. If you don't take yourself seriously, you'll struggle to begin your purpose. If you're not fully committed, it might mean you're not ready yet, and that's okay. You may need more time to figure things out before you decide to walk the path of your purpose.

Do you understand what it takes to pursue your purpose? It's crucial to understand what pursuing your purpose really involves. If you don't, you might have a false idea of what it's going to be like. Know that this journey might mean losing close friends, separating from loved ones who don't align with your purpose, or even ending long-term relationships. Pursuing your purpose can bring disappointment, pain, frustration, and sometimes loneliness. As long as you're prepared for these realities, you'll be better equipped to handle them.

What price are you willing to pay to fulfil your purpose? Everything in life comes with a price, and it's not always about money. Before you start, you need to be clear about the price you're willing to pay. This could be the loss of relationships, comfort, or even personal sacrifices. The bigger the purpose, the bigger the price. Think about historical figures who paid the ultimate price for their cause—they understood the risks and still chose to move forward. So, ask yourself, "What price am I willing to pay to fulfil my purpose?" and be honest with your answer.

What changes are you willing to make in your life to align with your purpose? To fulfil your purpose, you must be ready to make the necessary changes to properly align yourself with the higher-level duties you wish to fulfil. You can't be on your purpose if you're not willing to make those changes. It's like saying you want a job but not bothering to look for one—it just doesn't add up. Let's look at how you can start making changes in your life that will align with your purpose.

- **Evaluate the Toxic People in Your Life**

To make the changes needed to align with your purpose, you must start by evaluating the people in your life who are toxic. Being surrounded by toxic individuals will only hinder your progress; their negativity is like a disease that can spread and infect you. You won't be able to fully pursue your purpose until you distance yourself from toxic people—they will only hold you back and create barriers. In many cases, these toxic people might be those closest to you, such as family or long-time friends, but even so, you must decide whether to distance yourself from them in order to fulfil your purpose.

- **Remove Toxic People Immediately**

Once you've identified the toxic individuals in your life, you need to start removing them with immediate effect. This can be difficult for many, as it often involves letting go of people you care about or childhood friends you've known for years. The challenge lies in the familiarity you have with these people and the fear of starting anew, especially with the uncertainty of building a new network that aligns with your purpose. This fear is why many hold on to toxic surroundings—not because they see value in them, but because they worry about whether new connections will work out. In times of doubt, trust that the process will work itself out, as long as you are conscious and deliberate in building your new, positive surroundings. Removing toxic people from your life will enable you to better serve your purpose and move forward on your path.

- **Assess Potential Barriers to Your Purpose**

To truly fulfil your purpose, it's crucial to identify any potential barriers that might stand in your way. These barriers could range from your own personal issues, the people you surround yourself with, or even someone you're in a relationship with—any of these could potentially hinder your progress. Your job might also be a barrier, especially if it lacks the flexibility you need to pursue your purpose. In such a case, you may need to consider leaving your job. However, it's essential to carefully plan your exit strategy so that you don't find yourself having to return to it once you've made the decision to leave. Remember, once you commit to your purpose, there's no going back to the mediocre life you once led. If you don't remove these barriers, they will ultimately remove you from your path, pulling you away from your purpose.

• **Create New Healthy Habits to Replace Old Dysfunctional Ones**

We are all creatures of habit, whether those habits are good or bad. To fulfil your purpose effectively, you need to evaluate your current habits and assess them honestly. If you identify any dysfunctional habits that could hinder your ability to live out your purpose, it's time to replace them with healthier, more beneficial ones. The first step is to acknowledge that these dysfunctional habits exist and admit that they are problematic for your life and pose a threat to your purpose. Once you've accepted this, it's time to take action and form new, healthier habits that will support and enhance your journey towards fulfilling your purpose.

#12 - Replace Individualism with a Unifying Philosophy

In today's society, many of us live by individualism rather than coming together as a community and supporting each other. This mindset has become the norm, leading to a "dog eat dog" mentality where everyone is out for themselves. Individualism has made people more selfish, creating a culture of isolation. This way of living has resulted in many people suffering in silence, without anyone around to help them correct the errors in their lives.

There are countless individuals struggling with serious mental health issues while still managing to go about their daily routines —working, shopping, going to the gym, taking holidays— appearing fine on the surface. But when you get to know them better, you might notice some deeply concerning issues lurking beneath. The lack of community and support has left them to deal with these problems on their own, often with no one to turn to for help.

This is the downside of individualism—it breeds selfishness and a lack of awareness or concern for others. People become so focused on themselves that they become oblivious to the struggles of those around them. To truly thrive in Babylon, we need to shift away from this mindset and embrace a unifying philosophy.

Some might wonder why they should bother uniting with others when they can manage on their own, avoiding the potential hassles and disappointments that come with relying on others. But if you live by that philosophy, you'll eventually reach a point where you burn out. There's only so much you can achieve on your own. If you aspire to accomplish great things in life, you'll need the support of others.

Building a healthy future for your family and future generations requires a unifying philosophy. It takes the collective effort of parents, extended family, and even the wider community, all working together despite any differences. Petty disagreements must be set aside for the greater good, allowing unity to become the foundation for lasting success.

When you look at the state of society and our communities today, you have to wonder how things got this bad. Most people are stuck in survival mode, doing whatever they feel like with little to no accountability. The younger generation is running wild because they feel like no one cares about them, leaving them with no sense of belonging in their communities or society as a whole. This is why Babylon is falling and will keep falling—because no one wants to help one another. We live in a transactional society where people only connect with you if you have something they want. This kind of thinking comes from individualism, where everyone is just out for themselves.

It's understandable why individualism is so common in today's world. When you wake up every day to a world where people don't seem to care about you, your family, or your struggles, it can make you cold and force you into looking out for yourself because no one else will. But the thing you might not realise is that by acting selfishly, like everyone else, you become just like those you criticise. Instead of breaking the cycle of selfishness, you end up contributing to it.

The unifying philosophy encourages you to break that cycle by being more selfless rather than selfish. Working together with others, instead of trying to do everything on your own, allows you to achieve much more. The unifying philosophy isn't just about helping others; it's about realising that we can all achieve greater things together. So, be open to working with others and accepting help when it's offered. Shying away from this might only harm you in the long run.

We've often been told to surround ourselves with like-minded people, but the real question is: where do we find them? It's not like we live in a society where there's a specific place to meet people who think just like us. That idea might seem a bit unrealistic, but there's some truth to it as well. We have to recognise that we live in a scattered society, where people who share the same values and mindset are spread out and not easy to find because everything feels so disorganised. Because of this, instead of looking for these people in specific places, we need to think about how we can attract them to us, no matter where we are.

- **You need to be living by or working towards the unifying philosophy**

If you want to attract others to the unifying philosophy, you need to be living it yourself or at least in the process of transitioning towards it. When you're on this path, you'll naturally draw in people who are on the same journey. This shared direction can bring you and those like-minded individuals together.

- **Focus your energy on attracting people with a similar mindset**

While you're on your mission to find others who share your way of life, it's essential to focus your energy on attracting those types of people. Look for those who are either already living or are open to the unifying philosophy. It's also important to distance yourself from those who are committed to individualism, as they won't contribute to the collective mindset you're aiming for.

- **Be prepared to build with those who share the unifying philosophy**

The essence of living by the unifying philosophy is being ready to unite and work with others who are on the same path. When you find like-minded people, be prepared to build and create something meaningful together.

- **Have a clear blueprint for the unifying philosophy**

Living by the unifying philosophy requires a clear plan or set of principles to follow. Having this blueprint makes it easier to explain the philosophy to others and can help attract people to it, as they will see that there's a clear and structured path to follow.

The message in this chapter is about how crucial it is to move away from individualism and embrace a unifying philosophy. Even though we live in a society where most people are selfish, cutthroat, and only look out for themselves, it's important not to fall into that mindset. In the long run, that way of thinking doesn't do you any favours. Always keep the unifying principle in mind and be ready to apply it whenever the opportunity arises.

CHAPTER 7

HOW TO BE ONE STEP AHEAD IN BABYLON

One of the key elements to surviving in Babylon is to always stay one step ahead. The Babylon system is constantly planning ahead, pushing agendas designed to keep you in a disadvantaged position. They plan far in advance, so it's crucial for us, as average people, to start doing the same—planning and staying a step ahead. By doing this, you can gain some leverage in your life, rather than being stuck on the hamster wheel.

Many of us struggle to get ahead in this Babylon system because we're not operating on our own timeline; we're living on someone else's schedule. This limited, mediocre lifestyle that Babylon imposes on us isn't beneficial for our growth as human beings—it only benefits those at the top. While we toil away at the bottom of the Babylon hierarchy, they stay on top, getting richer, while we, the majority, grow poorer and remain in a subordinate position.

Let's explore a few steps on how to get ahead in Babylon:
#1 - Create your own reality

To get ahead in Babylon, it's essential to start by creating your own reality that works in your favour. The reality we currently live in isn't one we've chosen; it's been imposed on us by the Babylon system, keeping us down while they remain on top. But how do you create your own reality within an already existing one?

First, ask yourself: what does reality mean to you? What kind of life do you want to lead each day? Rather than focusing on the day-to-day details, think about the principles you want to guide your life. Do you have a living philosophy that you want to follow?

It's important to understand how to create a new reality within the one that Babylon has set up for us. This can be tricky, as most people only know the Babylon way of living—working, going home, relaxing, sleeping, and then repeating the cycle. Introducing a new way of life to those unfamiliar with it can be challenging. You must be careful not to confuse the lines between the reality you want to create and the one that Babylon has established.

Some people have attempted to create their own reality but have gone to such extremes that they lose touch with themselves and others, leading to a state of delusion. This can harm your mental health and cause you to isolate yourself, thinking that others are the problem when the issue may be that your new reality isn't properly aligned with yourself or society. The reality you create must be practical, something you can apply in everyday life and take with you wherever you go. If it isn't, you might end up living in a false reality that brings more harm than good.

Here are some steps to help you create your own reality within the Babylon system:
- Gain knowledge of yourself.
- Have confidence in your abilities to make it happen.
- Be determined and brave enough to shape your own reality.
- Draft a theoretical blueprint of how you want to live.
- Test this blueprint over a period of time to see if it works in the real world.
- If your tests are successful, you can then implement an official blueprint that you and others can follow.

#2 - Recreate yourself

To get ahead in Babylon, it's crucial to recognise that you might need to recreate yourself at some point. The reason for this is that from childhood to adulthood, much of your mindset, attitudes, and beliefs have likely been shaped by Babylon, whether you're aware of it or not. From your early years in nursery and primary school, through to secondary school, college, and university, the system has had an influence on how you perceive yourself and those around you. Babylon isn't just a system; it's also a society shaped and controlled by the system itself. The way of life presented to you daily is steeped in Babylonian ideals.

Recreating yourself is a necessary step because it gives you the opportunity to re-evaluate who you are and break free from the mental chains placed on you by the system and the environment you live in. This process allows you to build a new and improved version of yourself, one that can rise above the limitations that society imposes on you.

By recreating yourself, you can gain several benefits that will help you stay one step ahead in Babylon:
- Repair any damage you've encountered on your life's journey.
- Strengthen your character.
- Upgrade the quality of your thinking.
- Improve the overall quality of your life.

Recreating yourself isn't just about personal growth; it's about survival. It allows you to shed old habits and develop new, healthier ones that align with the best version of yourself. This transformation is essential if you want to not only survive but thrive in a society that often works against you.

#3 - Revolutionise Your Mind

Revolution, in this context, means bringing about change, so by revolutionising your mind, you can transform the way you think, the way you act, and even how you view life. It's essential because Babylon has a way of brainwashing and distracting people, keeping them from thinking independently. Babylon has people's minds in a chokehold, so the only way to free your mind is to revolutionise it. This new way of thinking will give you the edge you need to stay ahead in this system.

#4 - Invest Time in Yourself

Consider the time you spend going to work every day. Think about the hours you invest in watching TV shows, Netflix, Amazon Prime, endless YouTube videos, or scrolling through social media. Now, ask yourself, how much time are you investing in yourself? How much of your time is spent on work, others, or distractions? If you want to get ahead in Babylon, investing time in yourself is crucial. There are many ways you can do this—going to the gym, reading a book that will help you gain the knowledge you need to develop further, or simply using your spare time to plan your next steps in life. Remember, Babylon is designed to make you invest time into its way of life, keeping you from investing in your own. But if you want to break free from the hamster wheel and move forward, it's vital to start investing time in yourself.

#5 - Surround Yourself with Wise People

If you want to get ahead in Babylon, it's smart to surround yourself with people who have wisdom. Keep in mind that wise people don't always have all the answers, as they too are constantly learning from life. However, they can offer you valuable insights, good advice, and fresh perspectives that you might not have considered. They can guide you in making decisions that positively impact your life. Unfortunately, we live in a society where guidance is often lacking due to the breakdown of families, leading many young people to make poor choices. This lack of direction has resulted in a society with little order. Wisdom is in short supply in this Babylon system, which is why it's so crucial to have wise people around you. They help keep you sharp, alert, and thoughtful in the decisions you make. Remember, the system is designed to limit your ability to think critically, maintaining a state of chaos and disruption so those in power can stay on top. Surrounding yourself with wise individuals will help you navigate and get ahead in this society.

#6 - Listen to Those with More Life Experience

Another key to getting ahead in Babylon is to listen to those who have more life experience than you. This doesn't mean they're always right, but it does mean they have a wealth of knowledge to offer because of what they've lived through. It's unwise to dismiss the advice of someone who has seen more of life than you have. Yet, some people in society arrogantly believe they know it all, even when they lack the experience or understanding to back it up. Those with more life experience can teach you the do's and don'ts of life because they've already been through it. By learning from their experiences, you can avoid making the same mistakes and make better decisions for yourself. This kind of learning can help you get ahead because you won't have to suffer the consequences that others have, simply because you listened and took their advice.

In closing, if you're serious about getting ahead in Babylon, you need to put in the extra work on yourself. The system isn't designed for you to rise above it; it's designed to keep you in a subservient position. The government's education system, for instance, doesn't teach you to think for yourself—it teaches you to be a worker for them, to build their empire while you stay at the bottom.

Part II

THE WORKPLACE

CHAPTER 8

HOW TO CARRY YOURSELF

In this chapter, we'll talk about how to carry yourself in the workplace while quietly working towards becoming a better version of yourself. If you have bigger plans for your future and don't want to be stuck in a job until retirement, this chapter will guide you on how to manage that until your dreams start to take shape. Remember, the goal is to survive and thrive in Babylon, so we need to be strategic and think carefully about every move we make at work.

When it comes to how you carry yourself at work, it's important to always stay professional. This might sound obvious, but as many people know, professionalism can often slip in the Western workforce. Some people get too comfortable at work, which is understandable since they spend so much time there—five days a week, over 30 hours a week, with the same people. Naturally, they start building relationships with their colleagues, which leads to a level of comfort. However, getting too comfortable can lead to lapses in professionalism. Always remember that you're there to do a job, not to get too cosy.

When you're around your colleagues, try to stay neutral and treat everyone the same, regardless of their personalities. Avoid getting involved in workplace cliques. Many people fall into this trap, but it can be a mistake. Being part of a clique can put you in a compromised position and might cause your peers to label you as part of that particular group. By staying neutral, you allow yourself to move freely around the workplace without being pigeonholed into different social groups.

Carry yourself in a balanced way. It's fine to have a laugh and joke with your colleagues, but don't let that become your main interaction. You want your colleagues to take you seriously, and if they get too comfortable with you, they might blur the lines of what's appropriate. Maintaining a professional distance ensures that you're respected and keeps you focused on your long-term goals.

When it comes to how you carry yourself in the workplace, I like to think of it as following something I call the Modern Workforce Philosophy (MWP). This philosophy covers the basics of how to navigate today's work environment effectively. It includes the following principles:

#1 - Be easy to work with In the workplace

It is smart to make yourself easy to work with. When you're approachable and cooperative, people are more likely to enjoy working with you, whether it's on projects or daily tasks. Being easy to work with can make your workday smoother since your colleagues will appreciate your positive and flexible attitude, making collaborations much more pleasant.

#2 - Focus on getting the job done

At work, your main focus should always be on getting the job done, no matter what. Even when things get tough and the workload starts to pile up, it's important to stay focused. Break down your tasks into smaller, manageable sections and tackle them one at a time. Don't let the overall size of the workload overwhelm you—just concentrate on the next step. The key idea here is that if you stay focused on completing your tasks, you'll find a way to get through them.

#3 - Work with your colleagues, not against them

In the workplace, some people can make things difficult for

others by not cooperating or following team protocols. This can feel like they're working against you rather than with you. Even if you don't always agree with your colleagues or particularly like them, it's important to put those feelings aside and work together to get the job done. It's not about personal preferences; it's about teamwork and achieving the common goal.

#4 - Be open to learning from your colleagues

It's always beneficial to learn from the people you work with. By doing so, you can improve your skills and become more effective in your job. You might pick up new techniques or insights that could be useful in the long run. Being open to learning from your colleagues also helps you stay in sync with them, creating a positive and productive work environment for everyone.

#5 - Focus on finding solutions

When issues come up at work, it's important to stay focused on finding solutions rather than dwelling on the problem. Some colleagues might spend time complaining, which doesn't help resolve anything. Instead, keep a solution-oriented mindset so that when challenges arise, you're prepared to tackle them head-on and keep things moving forward.

#6 - Be versatile and adaptable

In the workplace, it's crucial to be versatile and adaptable. This means being flexible in how you communicate with different colleagues, who may come from various cultures and backgrounds. Since you'll be spending a lot of time with these people, it's smart to find common ground and create a positive working relationship with each of them. Developing a versatile approach to dealing with different colleagues will make your day-to-day work life much smoother.

It's also important to adapt to any changes that come up at work. Don't be rigid in your approach—be open to working with different people and adjust to the various personalities you encounter. Failing to adapt can lead to discomfort and stress in your work life, so it's essential to embrace an adaptable mindset. Remember, adapting your character doesn't mean being fake; it's about adjusting your approach to fit the work environment you're in.

#7 - Get along with everyone, even if you don't like them

To work successfully with your colleagues five days a week, you'll need to get along with everyone, even if you don't like them personally. Remember, you're not at work to make friends; you're there to do a job. Keep your focus on that, and don't let personal feelings toward colleagues distract you. It's all about maintaining a respectful working relationship, which is all you really need to get through each day smoothly. Any other relationship you form outside of work is a separate matter and usually not work-related.

How you carry yourself at work is very important. Your survival there depends on how you handle things daily—staying calm, rational, keeping your emotions in check, and focusing on getting the job done.

CHAPTER 9

KEEP YOUR PERSONAL LIFE PRIVATE

When you're at work, it's important to recognise how sharing your personal business can impact your job. We've all heard the saying, "Don't mix business with pleasure," and it's pretty straightforward. Mixing the two rarely ends well and can be detrimental to your work life, so it's crucial to keep them separate.

I understand that we spend a lot of time with our colleagues, so it's natural to form relationships where you might share personal information from time to time. This can build trust and make your colleagues feel more comfortable around you. However, it's essential not to overshare, as revealing too much about your personal life can harm your professional reputation. Some people make the mistake of disclosing too much, which might lead colleagues to comment on or even critique your personal life without fully understanding the context.

For instance, sharing relationship problems at work is generally unwise. Some colleagues might take that information and gossip about it, spreading your personal business around the office. Your private life should remain just that—private—and not be a topic of conversation among coworkers. In some cases, confiding in a colleague of the opposite sex about relationship issues can lead to an affair, especially if that colleague has had feelings for you and sees an opportunity to get closer. This can complicate things further, and the person you confide in might not have your best interests at heart, potentially sabotaging your relationship.

This is why it's so important not to divulge too much personal information at work. The workplace is not a therapy session, and bringing your personal problems into the office could make you the subject of gossip. Additionally, your colleagues might misinterpret aspects of your personal life, leading to misunderstandings and potentially harming your professional image.

Always try to keep conversations at work focused on work-related topics. Anything outside of that should remain private, ensuring you maintain clear boundaries between your professional and personal life.

CHAPTER 10

YOUR COLLEAGUES ARE NOT YOUR FRIENDS

In the workplace, it's important to remember that your colleagues are not your friends. Some people mistakenly think they are because, over the years, they've been invited to social events like going to the pub, attending a colleague's birthday party, or even going camping together. Engaging in fun activities outside of work can create a bond that feels more personal, so I understand why you might think of your colleagues as friends. You may have shared a few personal things about yourself during these outings, and you might have seen a different side of your colleagues—one that's more relaxed and less professional. This can give the impression of friendship when you see aspects of their personal character outside of work.

However, despite these experiences, I'm sorry to say that your colleagues are still just your colleagues, not your friends. Let's explore why they won't ever be true friends:

• They don't owe you friendship; they are simply your colleagues.

• The workplace is a forced environment where you don't choose who you work with.

• When dealing with personal issues outside of work, your colleagues aren't obligated to help, as it's not their concern.

• If a colleague is competing with you for a promotion, they might do whatever it takes, regardless of any so-called friendship.

• When you leave your job, you might not stay in contact with your colleagues.

- You may not even want to be around your colleagues outside of working hours.

Looking at these points, it becomes clearer why your colleagues aren't your friends. You weren't hired to make friends; you were hired to do a job and contribute to the organisation's success. It's in your best interest to focus on your work and not feel obligated to do anything beyond that.

CHAPTER 11

AVOID DISCUSSING YOUR POLITICAL VIEWS AT WORK

When it comes to discussing politics at work, it's wise to tread carefully. The workplace is not the best environment to dive into deep political discussions, especially if your views don't align with the mainstream. Most of your colleagues likely have a surface-level understanding of politics, and many of them aren't particularly interested in discussing it in depth. Bringing up strong political opinions, especially those that differ from the commonly accepted ones, can create tension and awkwardness, which is something you'd probably want to avoid.

If your political views lean towards the radical, extreme, or just significantly different from what your colleagues might think, it's a good idea to keep those opinions to yourself while you're at work. Expressing such views can easily offend others, especially in today's workplace, where political correctness is taken very seriously. Political correctness has been introduced to create a more harmonious working environment by limiting conversations that could be deemed controversial or offensive. This means that voicing opinions that step outside these boundaries can land you in hot water, potentially causing problems with colleagues or even management.

It's essential to remember that you weren't hired to share your political beliefs; you were brought in to do a specific job. Your role in the workplace is to contribute to the team and the company's objectives, not to engage in political debates. If you do start sharing political ideas that don't fit with the workplace culture, you risk raising red flags. Your colleagues might feel uncomfortable, or worse, they might report your views to higher management. This could put your job at risk, and in extreme cases, could even lead to disciplinary action or dismissal.

In today's working world, keeping your job and ensuring a smooth working experience means being aware of these potential pitfalls. It's easy to slip into a conversation about current events or politics, especially with so much happening in the world. But before you know it, a casual comment could spiral into a heated discussion that doesn't do you any favours.

It's also worth noting that political discussions at work rarely lead to anything productive. Most people are pretty set in their ways when it comes to politics, and trying to change someone's mind in a professional setting is usually a losing battle. Instead of building bridges, these discussions often create divisions. And in a place where teamwork and cooperation are crucial, the last thing you want to do is create unnecessary tension.

So, the smart move is to focus on your work and keep conversations professional. If someone else brings up politics, it's okay to steer the conversation back to work-related topics or to remain neutral. You can always say something like, "I prefer to keep work and politics separate," and then move on. This approach not only keeps you out of trouble but also helps maintain a peaceful and productive work environment.

CHAPTER 12

BE STOIC

Stoic philosophy can be a helpful approach in the workplace, especially when you need to navigate challenging situations. Being stoic doesn't mean you don't have emotions; it means you've learned how to manage and control them without letting them show. Imagine you're having a particularly hectic day at work, where the stress levels are high, and the pressure is on from start to finish. In these situations, you might notice that some of your colleagues start to crack under the pressure because they struggle with stress. But for you, it's important not to follow the same path of reacting emotionally or lashing out, as that kind of behaviour can create a ripple effect of stress among your colleagues who are simply trying to get their work done.

Being stoic is about thinking and acting rationally, staying responsive rather than reactive. To apply stoic philosophy effectively at work, you need to be stable within yourself. If you're someone who struggles with anger or other emotional challenges, the stoic approach might not come naturally to you. In fact, it may not work at all unless you've first taken steps to address and heal those emotional instabilities. Stoic philosophy requires a certain level of inner calm and balance, which might mean you need to focus on some personal healing before you can fully embrace this mindset.

Let's explore some basic therapeutic steps you might need to take to prepare yourself for applying stoic philosophy in the workplace.

#1 - Healing from past traumas

To embrace the stoic philosophy, it's important to heal from past traumas. Healing doesn't mean forgetting what happened, but rather accepting that these experiences are now part of who you are. The key is to make peace with these past events and find harmony within yourself. Peace is essential for stoic thinking because this philosophy is all about bringing a sense of calm and balance to any situation.

#2 - Managing triggers that affect your behaviour

To practice stoicism, you need to manage the triggers that might cause you to react impulsively. If you find yourself often reacting strongly to certain situations or people, this is something that needs attention. Instead of reacting immediately when triggered, take a moment to pause and consider how you can respond calmly. The stoic approach is about not being controlled by your triggers but learning to control your responses to them.

#3 - Unlearning unhealthy thinking habits

The stoic philosophy encourages rational and logical thinking. To maintain a healthy mindset, it's important to unlearn any unhealthy thinking habits that may cause unnecessary problems. For example, you might think that if a child consistently misbehaves, they must be a bad person. In reality, the child may simply be misguided and in need of guidance. By changing how you think about the child, you could help teach them to behave better. Unhealthy thinking habits could include always expecting the worst in a situation rather than seeing the potential positives. To effectively use stoic philosophy, you must unlearn any habits that prevent you from thinking rationally and logically. A quick exercise is to recall a situation where you struggled to think rationally. Identify the unhealthy thinking habits that held you back and then start the process of unlearning them, one step at a time.

#4 - Consider the possible domino effect of your actions on others

Before reacting in the workplace, it's important to consider the potential domino effect your actions could have on others. Stoic philosophy teaches us to think first before reacting. Consider the conflicts your actions could cause, the disruptions they might bring, and how others might react. Be mindful of the impact your actions can have on those around you. If you tend to react impulsively, it might be time to develop a habit of thinking before you act. Make it a daily practice until it becomes second nature.

In this chapter, I hope you've gained a clear understanding of what it means to be stoic and why this philosophy is so valuable in the workplace. It's essential for maintaining a steady and composed approach while working with your colleagues. However, remember that to practice stoicism effectively, you need to be mentally and emotionally stable, or the philosophy won't serve you well.

CHAPTER 13

———

STICK TO THE SCRIPT

In the workplace, it's important to create a consistent way of interacting with your colleagues—a "script," if you like. Once you've established this script, it's crucial to stick to it. Your colleagues will come to identify you by the way you consistently behave, and if you suddenly change how you act, it can throw them off. They've become used to the version of you that you've presented, and flipping the script might disrupt the harmony in the workplace.

When I say "stick to the script," I mean you should maintain the character you've shown to your colleagues from the start. It's important to stay true to this character so that you can work peacefully with everyone. You don't want to cause any disruptions that could affect how smoothly things run. Some people start a new job by being overly nice because they want to be accepted by their colleagues. But once they feel comfortable, they might think it's okay to start acting differently. What they don't realise is that changing the way they behave can lead to distrust among their colleagues. The script you begin with should be the one you stick to.

Think of it like an actor following a script in a film. The actor has to read the lines exactly as they're written. If they start improvising, they'll be told to stop and go back to the script. If they keep changing the lines, it disrupts the process of making the film. The same goes for the workplace—you need to stick to the script of how you want your colleagues to see you. For example, if you start out as someone who's always cooperative, that's what your colleagues will expect from you. You'll need to keep up with that script because it's how you've presented yourself.

The goal in the workplace is to maintain a consistent script that makes it easy for your colleagues to work with you. This consistency helps ensure that everyone can get their work done efficiently, keeping things running smoothly day after day.

CHAPTER 14

———

AVOID GOSSIP

Talking about other employees behind their backs at work isn't a smart move. It's important to remember that you were hired to do a job, not to spread rumours. Engaging in gossip at work can backfire on you, as you might end up being held accountable for any misinformation or personal details you've shared. If you're regularly gossiping, you're putting yourself at risk of unnecessary conflicts. For instance, if a colleague confides in you, and you go on to share that information with others, you're betraying their trust. What you might not have considered is how that colleague will react if they find out you've been spreading their private information.

Gossiping can lead to a breakdown in trust. If your colleagues know you're quick to talk about others, they won't feel comfortable sharing anything with you. For a workplace to function smoothly, colleagues need to trust each other. A certain level of confidentiality is needed to protect everyone's reputation. If you become known as the office gossip, you're not only risking your job, but also creating tension with those you work with.

Imagine if a colleague finds out you've been gossiping about them. They might keep working with you because they have to, but underneath, they could be holding a grudge. This could lead to a situation where they no longer trust you, and the good working relationship you once had could be ruined. The tension between you might make it difficult to work together effectively, all because you couldn't resist the urge to spread gossip instead of focusing on your work.

The best approach when someone tries to draw you into gossip is simply not to engage. You can acknowledge what they're saying with a nod, but don't contribute to the conversation. They'll soon realise that you're not interested in participating, and they'll likely move on to someone else. The key takeaway is to avoid gossiping at work at all costs, or you might face negative consequences from the colleagues you've been talking about.

CHAPTER 15

UNDERSTANDING HOW THE WORKPLACE OPERATES

Understanding how things work in the workplace is crucial. It helps you navigate interactions with your colleagues and shows you the right and wrong ways to act at work. Let's explore a few key points you should keep in mind about how your workplace operates:

#1 - Workplace Politics

Understanding the politics of your workplace is essential for navigating your role effectively. For example, modern workplaces often have strict guidelines around communication, especially regarding what's considered politically correct. You need to be mindful of how you express your views. For instance, making a comment like "women shouldn't take leadership roles because they're too emotional" would be seen as offensive and politically incorrect. Similarly, voicing disapproval of gay or lesbian relationships at work could land you in serious trouble, as most workplaces have strict policies against discrimination based on race, gender, religion, or beliefs. If your personal views don't align with the accepted norms of workplace communication, it's best to keep them to yourself to avoid negative repercussions on your job.

It's also important to understand the hierarchy and power dynamics within your workplace, from the head of the department and managers down to the junior staff. Knowing these dynamics helps you navigate your work environment more smoothly and ensures you communicate appropriately with your colleagues, staying within the bounds of political correctness. Understanding the politics of your workplace will guide you on how to operate effectively and maintain a positive, professional atmosphere.

#2 - Observe How Your Colleagues Operate at Work

In the workplace, it's crucial to pay attention to how your colleagues operate on a daily basis. Notice how they communicate with each other, how they handle stress when under pressure, and how sensitive each colleague is. Also, try to understand how your colleagues think, but remember, your personal feelings about their mindset are irrelevant when your goal is to understand how they function. By grasping how your colleagues operate, you can interact with them more effectively. For instance, when you see colleagues under stress, some might react strongly due to the pressure they're experiencing. If you've observed how they typically respond to stress, you'll know the best way to approach them during those moments.

Another example is dealing with sensitive colleagues. If someone is particularly sensitive, you'll need to be mindful of the kind of jokes or comments you make around them. Sometimes colleagues joke around with each other and can unintentionally cross a line. While one person might try to laugh it off, they could be upset underneath. This kind of situation can lead to tension in the workplace. Your role is to understand what you can and can't say to avoid offending someone. After all, you work with these people every day, and creating a positive atmosphere is important. The key message here is that by studying your colleagues, you gain valuable insight into how to interact with them, making your work environment smoother and more harmonious.

#3 - Professionalism in the Workplace

In your job, it's essential to observe the level of professionalism among your colleagues. Ask yourself, is the professionalism in your workplace up to a high standard? This isn't just about following the company's policies, but about really understanding how professional your colleagues are in their day-to-day behaviour. While modern workplaces often promote professionalism, you'll likely notice that some colleagues overstep these boundaries, and sometimes, they get away with it.

For example, a married person might come to work and start discussing their marital problems with others. No matter how you feel about that, it's unprofessional to do so. Consider this: when someone brings their personal issues to work, it can lead to gossip, which disrupts the professional environment. If you're having marital or personal issues, it's best to keep them separate from your work life.

Sometimes, people might show up to work in a bad mood, perhaps due to an argument on their way to work or because they're dealing with a personal issue. They might even take out their frustrations on someone at work. While it's understandable that everyone has bad days, if everyone brought their personal problems to work, it would severely impact how colleagues interact and get the job done. Emotions running high at work can create a tense atmosphere that hinders productivity and collaboration.

Understanding the level of professionalism in your workplace is crucial. It helps you navigate your work environment more effectively and gives you a better sense of the kind of organisation you're working for. Even if some colleagues occasionally step out of line, it's important that you don't follow suit. Always stay within the bounds of professionalism, no matter the situation. This will help you maintain your integrity and ensure that you're seen as a reliable and professional member of the team.

#4 - Handling Your Workload

Every job comes with its own daily workload, and when you first apply, the job description usually lists your main responsibilities. However, if you look closely, it often mentions that other duties may arise. This is something you'll need to accept, even if it's not ideal, because sometimes it's simply out of your control. For instance, if a colleague is off sick, you might have to step in and take on extra tasks. Managing your workload can be challenging, but there are ways to handle the pressure that comes with it.

i) Break the workload into manageable tasks

The first step in handling your workload is to break it down into smaller, more manageable tasks. Start by focusing on the most important tasks first, then move on to the less urgent ones afterward. This approach helps prevent you from feeling overwhelmed. Always remember to tackle your tasks one step at a time until they're completed. If you find that you couldn't finish everything within your planned time due to tight circumstances, try not to stress—it may be beyond your control. Just keep working steadily toward completing each task until they're all done.

ii) Work within your time frame:

Completing your workloads can be tiring and sometimes stressful, especially when you're on a tight deadline. However, you can only work within the time frame you have, even if your boss's expectations are unrealistic. For example, if you start work at 8:45 am and finish at 4:30 pm, that's your time frame.

You also need to consider your break times within those hours. The goal is to manage your workload within that time frame because that's all you can realistically do. Let's quickly review how your time frame is measured in the workplace:

- The time you start work
- Your break times
- The time you finish work

When we talk about working within your time frame, it's not just about meeting your boss's deadlines but also understanding the structure of your workday, including your start time, breaks, and finish time. If we think of it as a simple equation, your workday time frame is calculated as **start time + break time + finish time = determined workday workload time frame**. This means your start time determines when you begin your tasks, break time temporarily pauses your work, and finish time marks the end of your workday. Understanding this helps you manage your workload without overwhelming yourself, knowing that you only have a set amount of time to complete your tasks. To protect yourself as an employee, always ensure you're making progress on your tasks, even if delays occur. If you face setbacks, don't hesitate to talk to the person who assigned the tasks, explaining any issues that have arisen. This way, you might negotiate an extension or get extra support from colleagues to complete the job.

iii) Approach your workload with a sense of calmness

When you're dealing with your workload, no matter how heavy it may seem, it's best to approach it with a calm mindset. It's understandable that a large workload can sometimes feel overwhelming and stressful. However, if you let it get to you, it could negatively affect your mental health and overall wellbeing. Remember, trying to rush through your tasks won't lead to quality work. Let's explore some ways to approach your workload calmly:

- **Quality workload approach**

The quality workload approach is a strategy you can use to ensure you produce high-quality work while on the job. Instead of rushing to complete tasks quickly, consider slowing down and applying this method. When you rush, you're more likely to make critical mistakes, which could cost you time in the long run as you may need to go back and correct those errors. The quality workload approach is all about completing tasks with a focus on quality, which can save you from having to redo work later.

- **Steady approach**

The steady approach is about tackling your workload at a balanced pace—not too fast, not too slow. Using this method, you'll find that your tasks get completed in a consistent manner. You'll also notice that your stress levels are easier to manage, making your approach to work more positive. The steady approach, combined with a positive mindset, helps create a balanced flow, allowing you to complete your tasks efficiently while keeping stress at bay.

- **Non-pressure type of approach**

The non-pressure type of approach is a strategy that helps you minimise the pressure you feel while getting the job done efficiently. Even if you're under pressure, the key is not to dwell on it. Instead, focus on completing the task at hand. The more you concentrate on the pressure, the more stressed you'll become. On the other hand, the less you think about it, the easier it is to stay calm and focused. The non-pressure approach is all about keeping pressure to a minimum, avoiding unnecessary stress while you work through your tasks in the workplace.

Part III

RAISING YOUR CHILDREN

CHAPTER 16

———

RAISING YOUR CHILDREN IN BABYLON

In today's Babylonian era, it's clear that raising children is more challenging than ever. There are so many hurdles that come with parenting in the society we live in now. We see a lot of broken families who don't communicate, relatives who distance themselves from their own, and a high number of single-parent households. This often leads to an imbalance for children, as one parent bears the heavy load of responsibilities. Then there's the uncivilised behaviour among adults, which gets passed down to their children and spreads to others like a domino effect. Add to this the toxic influence of social media on young minds, the flawed education system that misguides our children, and the school environments that can also create challenges for parents during their child's upbringing.

These are just a few of the obstacles many parents face when raising children in today's Babylon. The goal of this chapter is to guide you through some basic steps on how to raise children in such a fractured society. We need to ask ourselves whether we can ever restore the traditional family structure that once existed or if it's time to create a new approach to raising our children in the situation we now face. That's a question for you to reflect on, as I already have my own answer. While you consider this, let's begin with the process of raising children in Babylon today:

#1 - Talk About Life Dynamics Before Having Children

If you're thinking about starting a family with your partner, it's crucial to have a conversation about how your current lifestyles might change before you make the decision to have children. Start by looking at your financial situation, as money plays a big role in raising a child. The cost of living keeps going up, and children can be quite expensive to care for. Having kids is a significant investment, requiring you to dedicate time, money, and resources to ensure your child grows up well and becomes a positive contributor to society.

Consider your family dynamics, particularly how much support you'll have from relatives if you decide to have children. For instance, if both you and your partner work during the day, you'll need someone to care for your child until you finish work. If you don't have family members available to help, daycare may be your only option, and that can be quite costly. Discussing these dynamics before having children is essential, as it allows both you and your partner to explore how life might change if you decide to start a family.

#2 - Talk About How You Want to Raise Your Child During Pregnancy

Bringing a child into the world is an exciting time for many, but it's important not to let that excitement distract you from having serious discussions about how you want to raise your child. A common mistake is waiting until the baby is born to start these conversations. Ideally, these discussions should happen during the pregnancy stage, allowing both parents to focus on adapting to the new life at home once the baby arrives.

Often, couples wait until after the baby is born to talk about parenting, only to discover later on that their views and principles on raising a child are quite different. This can lead to tension and disagreements, just when both parents should be bonding with the newborn and adjusting to the new routine. The early days of parenthood are already intense, exhausting, and sometimes stressful, and adding disagreements about parenting can make things even more challenging.

Having these important discussions during pregnancy is the wiser approach. It allows you to explore and understand each other's parenting ideals before the baby arrives, giving you time to work through any differences. If you do have disagreements about how to raise your child, it's better to resolve them before the baby is born. This way, when your child arrives, you can focus on adapting to parenthood without the added stress of conflicting views.

By discussing your approach to parenting early on, you set yourselves up for a smoother transition into your new roles as parents, with a shared vision and understanding of how you want to raise your child. This creates a more peaceful and harmonious environment for both the parents and the baby.

#3 - Choosing Your Child's Name

When it comes to naming your child, it's important to choose a name that carries meaning. Some people may not give much thought to the significance of a name, and that's their choice. However, for those who are serious about raising their child with a sense of purpose in today's world, finding a name with meaning is crucial.

Consider giving your child a name they can grow into, one that they can be proud of and aspire to live up to in the future. When your child is old enough to understand, take the time to explain the meaning behind their name and why it's important. By doing this, you're planting a seed in their mind that will eventually take root.

As they grow, your child may consciously or subconsciously begin to embody the qualities associated with their name. This simple act of naming can provide a strong foundation for raising them with purpose and intention. Choosing a meaningful name is more than just picking something that sounds nice; it's about giving your child something to strive towards, a name that reflects the values and aspirations you hope they will embrace as they grow.

#4 - Educating Your Children

When it comes to educating our children, it's something we should take very seriously. For years, we've been told to go to school, get a good education, and hopefully land a good job. That message might seem solid when you're a child, but as you step into the real world, you start to see that the basic education from school is quite limited. School education serves primarily as an academic tool, aimed mostly at securing a government job.

If this is the only kind of education your child has received, it's likely they won't reach their full potential because of the limited knowledge they've been exposed to. We need to understand that the schools we send our children to are designed in a way that keeps their thinking restricted. The people behind these schools don't want our children to outshine theirs; they don't want a new wave of innovators who might challenge their systems. So, they provide an average education that keeps our children's minds in a state of passivity.

This is where parents come in. It's up to us to take time out of our busy lives to give our children additional knowledge outside of school hours. If we want our children to succeed and go beyond the limited expectations set by the Babylon school system, we must offer them revolutionary education at home. Here's a brief list of educational areas you could explore with your child outside of school:

(i) Financial Literacy (Money)
Teaching your child financial literacy from an early age is

invaluable. These days, many people struggle with managing money, often because they haven't learned the basics. They tend to consume rather than invest. The goal here is to help our children understand how money works, teach them its value, and give them a basic understanding of assets and liabilities. You can also test your child's thinking by giving them scenarios to consider, like this one:

Question: If you had £2000, what would you spend it on? Your child's answer: . . . .

In the example above, you're asking your child to think about how they'd use £2000. If they respond with an answer that shows a consumer mindset, that's your cue to step in and guide them towards a more financially literate way of thinking. The idea is to help them see money as a tool, not just a means to buy luxuries.

Many people see money purely as something to spend—the more they have, the more they spend. This mindset often leads to poor financial decisions, regardless of how much money they actually have. By teaching your child financial literacy early on, you're equipping them with the skills to make wise financial choices as they grow older.

(ii) Politics

It's crucial to teach your children about politics, as many people today lack a solid understanding of how political systems work. By explaining politics to your child, you help them grasp how the country is run and how political decisions impact their everyday life—from schools and workplaces to the wider society they live in. You might consider getting them a book that covers the basics of politics and reading through it together. Over time, this will give them a better understanding of how politics influences their life, and it will equip them with the knowledge to navigate the complexities of the Babylon system.

(iii) Philosophy

Introducing your child to philosophy is a great way to help them develop critical thinking skills that will serve them well throughout their life. Philosophy encourages children to think deeply and ask questions. The goal of teaching your child philosophy is to help them question the information they receive, particularly in school, where the Babylon education system often presents a limited or skewed version of certain aspects of life. By giving your child even a basic understanding of philosophy, you're equipping them to think critically and independently.

A philosophical mindset trains your child to think for themselves, to question what they are told, and to develop their own ideas. With your guidance, they can learn to apply these concepts in their daily life, fostering independence in their thoughts and actions. This, in turn, will help them grow into individuals who are not easily swayed by others but who are confident in their ability to think and act independently.

(iv) Business

Introducing your child to the basics of business gives them a glimpse into how the world operates, even if it's just at a basic level. The truth is, most children today don't learn about business in school because it's not part of the curriculum. It's ironic that children attend school five days a week without realising that the very school they go to is, in fact, a business. The secondary school they attend is also a business, yet they leave without knowing it's a business establishment. Whether you're aware of it or not, your child is a business asset for the schools they attend, contributing to the school's economic gain. So why not teach them about the business side of the society they live in? When children learn about business early on, they start to understand how the real world functions—after all, we live in a business-driven world. They'll grasp that the world doesn't just operate on its own, and by learning about business early, they might even develop an entrepreneurial mindset.

For parents who feel they don't have the time to sit down and teach their child at home, I understand the busy schedules many parents have daily. But if you think you don't have the time, here's a potential solution: try setting aside just 20-30 minutes a week to educate your child on something that will benefit them in the future. Consider this: there are 10,080 minutes in a week, and 1,440 minutes in a day. I'm suggesting that out of those 1,440 minutes a day—or the 10,080 minutes in a week—you take just 20-30 minutes to provide some extra education at home. This small investment of time can give your child a better start in their education. The idea is simple: the more your child knows, the better equipped they'll be to make informed decisions as they grow up.

#5 - Structure

It's crucial for children to have structure in the household. Without it, you may find yourself dealing with chaotic, disorderly, and rebellious behaviour. The disorganised nature of today's society has seeped into how people run their homes, often leading to a loss of control over their own children. A lack of structure is one reason why so many children in Western society struggle with following rules and maintaining order. Structure brings discipline, order, and civilised behaviour into a child's life. A good way to instill this in your child is by introducing them to what I like to call the "General versus Soldier" concept. Think of it as a military-style approach to structure.

Explain to your child the difference between a general and a soldier. The general is the leader, the one who gives orders, while the soldier follows those orders, even if they don't always agree. This concept creates a clear understanding of roles within the household, with you as the parent being the general and your child the soldier. The goal is for your child to recognise this dynamic and understand their role in following instructions.

If your child steps out of line, pull them aside and ask whether they've been a good soldier. By this point, your child should understand the soldier concept well enough to know if they've met your expectations. Structure is a powerful tool for bringing order to your child's daily life. When used consistently, it helps your child develop their own sense of organisation and discipline as they grow older.

#6 - Consistency

For a child to truly excel and achieve results in life, they need consistency in the home. As a parent, it's your responsibility to provide that consistency, helping your child develop habits they can rely on. For example, if you want your child to make their bed each morning, ensure you remind them to do it daily. They might forget at first, but with regular reminders, they'll eventually make it a habit they follow without needing to be told.

Another example is encouraging your child to clean up after themselves. If they make a mess at the dinner table, have them tidy it up each time. By consistently reinforcing this behaviour, your child will learn to do it on their own. Any routine you want your child to follow needs to be maintained consistently by you, so they can learn to be consistent in their actions as well.

Many parents today in Western society tend to do things when they feel like it rather than when they need to. For instance, a parent might think, "I don't feel like cleaning the house today," even though they have children watching their every move. If a parent only cleans when they feel like it, rather than consistently keeping the house tidy, this behaviour can rub off on the child. The child might then develop the same attitude, doing things only when they feel like it instead of when they should.

The purpose of instilling consistency in your child is to teach them the importance of routine and responsibility, even when they don't feel like it. It's about showing them that certain tasks need to be done regardless of their mood. As a parent, you must model this consistent behaviour, because if you don't, you might unintentionally set your child up for difficulties in life. Without consistency, your child could grow up struggling to meet responsibilities, becoming a burden to themselves and a disappointment to others.

Consider this: wouldn't you want your child's teacher to be consistent in their education, ensuring your child gets the best learning experience possible? As a parent, you should apply the same level of consistency at home, so your child behaves properly at school, allowing the teacher to focus on teaching. It's a partnership—consistency at home supports consistency in the classroom.

Instilling consistency in your child brings several key benefits to their character:
- Trust
- Reliability
- Stability

In an unstable world like the one we live in today, teaching your child consistency is a powerful way to help them grow into stable, reliable individuals. It's one of the essential components for success in anything they choose to pursue in life.

#7 - Child preparation

When raising your child in today's world, it's crucial to get them ready for the realities of life. It's up to parents to prepare their children both mentally and emotionally. The way a child is brought up will often shape how they navigate their future as they move through the various stages of growing up. Let's explore a few ways to help prepare your child for the society they're growing up in:

(i) Shaping their mindset

Shaping your child's mindset is essential, especially in today's society where they are exposed to all sorts of information—some good, some bad. The bad information can come from various sources, including schools and friends, and it may be passed on in a misleading way. Your child, not knowing better, might take this information as fact due to their limited understanding. That's why it's crucial to start influencing your child's mindset early on. Teach them to think before they act. While this won't be easy, with consistent effort, you'll see the seeds you're planting begin to take root. Patience is key here, as every child needs time to develop.

A big part of shaping your child's mindset involves fostering positive thinking. The goal is to help your child see themselves in a positive light. Highlight the positive aspects of their character and make them aware of these strengths. This awareness can build reassurance and encourage a positive attitude in everything they do as they grow. Another crucial aspect of shaping their mindset is how they perceive failure. When your child fails at something, teach them not to dwell on the failure but to understand that they have another chance to try again and succeed. This approach trains them to view failure not as a dead-end but as an opportunity to learn, improve, and come back stronger with the determination to succeed.

(ii) Raise your child with honesty

In today's world, where dishonesty seems to have taken hold of many people's lives, it's crucial for parents to raise their children with honesty. But what does it mean to raise a child with honesty? It means, as a parent, you should always be willing to tell your child the truth, even if it's uncomfortable or hurts their feelings in the moment. By raising your child with honesty, you help reduce any level of deceit in their life. For instance, if you notice a weakness in your child's character, it's important to point it out so they can recognise it. The next step is to guide them in turning that weakness into a strength. Even though your child might not want to hear it, telling them the truth is crucial. It's better to be honest than to let your child be held back by their own shortcomings.

It's also important to encourage your child to be honest. The idea of raising children with honesty includes recognising when a child admits to doing something wrong. Instead of reacting immediately, take a moment to appreciate their honesty, then address the situation with any necessary discipline. This approach teaches your child that it's okay to tell the truth, but also helps them understand that being honest comes with responsibilities.

In today's society, many people are trapped by their own lies, largely due to the dishonest environment we live in. Sadly, dishonesty has become a dominant force, with little emphasis on truth-telling. Therefore, it's essential to raise a new generation of children with honesty, to help restore a balance in truthfulness.

(iii) Build Character

Building character in your child is crucial. Character is

something every child should develop, as it helps them grow into confident and independent individuals. Without a strong sense of character, a child can easily be influenced by others, imitating whatever they see around them without truly understanding it. By building character in your child, you create a sense of security and self-confidence within them, which is especially important in today's society where many people seem to be just copies of each other due to a lack of individuality. When developing character in your child, here are a few key areas to focus on:

- **Morals:**

Sadly, we live in a world where morals seem to be in short supply. Every day, we see wrongdoings happening all around us, from adults and children alike. Many of these wrongs go unchecked, so it's crucial to teach children about morals from a young age. By instilling morals, we help shape them into civilised individuals who can interact with others in a positive way and take responsibility when they've done something wrong.

- **Principles:**

Teaching your child principles is essential, as it gives them a strong foundation to live by. Principles act as a set of guiding rules that help shape a meaningful life. Without them, a person's life can lack direction and purpose. Raising your child with principles builds a solid base for their character, helping them develop a strong belief system and behaviour that will serve them well in the long run.

- **Knowledge:**

Knowledge is a powerful tool in raising your child. Providing them with knowledge boosts their confidence and shapes their character. It's important to teach your child a broad range of knowledge that they can use to create positive outcomes in their life. The more knowledge your child has, the more options and ways of thinking they'll have access to. Knowledge is crucial to a child's growth and development. Without it, they're more vulnerable to misinformation, manipulation, and being misled by others. Think of knowledge as food for the mind—the less your child has, the more their mind will be starved. Without proper knowledge, they may struggle to make the right decisions for their own growth. As a parent, it's your responsibility to nourish your child's mind with knowledge if you want to see them succeed in life.

- **Discipline:**

Discipline is essential when raising a child in Babylon. Without it, your child may become unruly, disobedient, disrespectful, and rebellious. Discipline brings order and respect into your household. It teaches your child that there are rules and guidelines they need to follow, and they learn that stepping out of line will have consequences. As a parent, you also need to consider how your child behaves when they're not under your watch, such as when they're at school. You want to know that your child has enough discipline to follow instructions and behave appropriately, so they don't cause unnecessary stress for their teachers. Remember, teachers spend five days a week with your child, and they likely have their own families to care for after school. You don't want a teacher going home stressed because your child lacks discipline. It's vital that you provide proper home training, teaching your child what is and isn't acceptable behaviour. This not only fosters respect but also teaches your child responsibility and accountability for their actions.

(iv) Teach your child to think for themselves

Teaching your child to think for themselves is crucial in today's world. It gives them independence in their thoughts and encourages them to make thinking and using their mind a natural part of their daily routine. Many children today spend a lot of time playing video games or using iPads, and while there's nothing wrong with that in moderation, if it's all they're doing, they might develop a short attention span. They could struggle to use their mind effectively because they're not exercising their brain enough. When the brain isn't used much, it can slow down in processing thoughts. That's why it's important to regularly challenge your child's thinking. Ask them questions that prompt them to think, giving them the chance to develop their own thoughts. It's also helpful to have conversations with your child where you ask questions or even engage in friendly debates. This not only stimulates their brain but also helps them expand their thinking process, leading to the habit of thinking for themselves more regularly.

(v) Preparing Your Child for Society

As your child grows and starts to engage more with the world around them, it's crucial to prepare them for the society they'll be a part of. This means gradually exposing your child to the realities of the world outside your home. Some parents might hesitate to do this, wanting to shield their children from the negative aspects of society. While it's understandable that you want to protect your child, over-sheltering them can actually hinder their growth and development. It's important to strike a balance – not to expose them to everything too soon, but also not to keep them too insulated from the world. Overprotecting your child can lead to anxiety because they aren't given the chance to understand or cope with the environment they will eventually need to navigate. As you introduce your child to society, there are a few key things to consider:

- **Helping Your Child Interact with Others**

A key part of preparing your child for the world is teaching them how to interact with other children. This is where your child begins to build the foundation for how they will engage with others throughout their life. At this stage, your child will learn to speak respectfully to their peers and respond thoughtfully in conversations. The goal of developing your child's interaction skills is to set them up for successful communication as they grow older and eventually enter adulthood. It's essential that children start mastering these social skills early on, as it lays the groundwork for how they will connect with people throughout their lives.

• Guiding Your Child to Manage Their Emotions

As your child grows, it's crucial to help them learn how to manage their emotions in a healthy way. In today's society, many people struggle with emotional issues, so teaching your child to handle their feelings properly is essential. By guiding your child in this area, you're helping them become emotionally intelligent as they progress through different stages of life into adulthood. The goal of starting this process early is to set them up for the future, ensuring they know how to deal with their emotions effectively. Ultimately, you want to raise a child who grows into a well-balanced adult, capable of navigating their emotions smoothly and keeping emotional conflicts to a minimum.

• Teaching Your Child to Handle Hostile People

Unfortunately, when your child starts interacting with society, they will inevitably encounter hostile individuals. For example, your child might be playing in the park and come across another child who hasn't learned how to interact properly. In this situation, it's important for your child to recognise the uncivil behaviour from the other child, who may have no intention of being friendly. The key lesson to impart to your child is to walk away from the hostile situation before it potentially escalates. If you think that walking away is a sign of weakness, it's worth reconsidering. The goal here is for your child to recognise hostility and avoid it entirely, rather than engaging with it. By teaching this strategy early on, you're helping to shape your child's mindset and approach to dealing with hostility in a disciplined and healthy way. The idea is for your child to carry this lesson into adulthood, learning that just because others may act aggressively, they don't have to follow suit. They should understand that hostile behaviour comes with consequences, and the ultimate aim is to raise a well-mannered child who sets a positive example for others.

- **Teaching Your Child About the Society They Live In**

As your child starts to interact more with the world around them, it's essential to help them understand the society they're growing up in. There are some lessons that your child will learn through their own experiences, especially when they're out and about, interacting with different people. For example, your child might be playing with other children and come across a child who uses inappropriate language. If your child decides to tell the child's parent, only to find that the parent doesn't seem to care or even finds it amusing, this can be quite a shock for your child. They might come back to you, confused and upset, expecting that the parent would have taken action.

This is a good moment for you to explain the variety of parenting styles that exist in society. You can explain to your child that not all parents discipline their children in the same way, and unfortunately, some behaviours they encounter are learned directly from those parents. It's important to make your child aware that not all families will share the same values, and this is something they'll need to understand as they navigate the world.

Similarly, your child might notice people begging for money on the street. This could happen regularly, and it's natural for them to be curious about why people are in such situations. Again, this is an opportunity to gently explain the realities of life, helping your child to understand the different circumstances people face. It's not about making them fearful, but rather giving them a realistic view of the world, so they don't grow up sheltered and unprepared for the realities of life.

I know as a parent it's tempting to protect your child from the harsh realities of the world, and it's natural to want to shield them from anything that might upset them. However, we have to acknowledge that we can't protect them forever. They need to experience and understand the society they live in to navigate it successfully as they grow older. By teaching your child about the world around them, you're helping them build confidence and awareness, which will serve them well as they move through life independently. The goal is to ensure that as they grow up, they have a clear understanding of the society they're a part of, and they feel equipped to handle it with confidence.

- **Instilling Awareness of the Outside Environment.**

When I talk about teaching children to be aware of their surroundings outside the home, I'm thinking about helping them to observe and pay close attention to what's happening around them. It's important to guide your child in noticing the behaviours of everyday people when they're out and about. A great way to instil this awareness is by taking your child on regular walks. Not only is this good exercise for both of you, but it also gives your child a chance to observe how people behave in different situations.

When you're out walking with your child, make sure they're doing the following:

- Walking beside you or just in front of you
- Keeping their head up

Let me explain why these two things matter. Having your child walk close to you or in front of you means you can keep a close eye on them and ensure they're paying attention to where they're going. Keeping their head up is crucial because it helps them stay aware of what's happening around them. You want your child to develop the habit of observing their surroundings as they walk, rather than being distracted.

For example, if you see someone engrossed in their phone while walking, not paying attention to their surroundings, point it out to your child. Ask if they noticed how that person wasn't paying attention, especially when crossing the road. Then, discuss the potential dangers, like the possibility of that person being hit by a car because they were too distracted to notice oncoming traffic.

If your child understands the importance of road safety, they'll likely tell you that crossing the road while focused on a phone is dangerous. This is a perfect opportunity to teach your child about the importance of paying attention when they're outside, particularly near roads.

• To help your child develop this awareness, it's important that you model the same behaviour. Show them what it means to move with caution and awareness when you're out together. By seeing you practise this level of care, your child is more likely to follow suit.

• The goal of instilling this awareness is to help your child understand how people behave in public spaces and to prepare them to navigate those spaces safely. While you can't control what happens outside, you can control how you guide your child in becoming more aware and cautious when they're out in the world. This awareness will help them deal with the realities of the outside environment, some of which may not always be pleasant but are important for them to recognise.

CHAPTER 17

CO-PARENTING IN BABYLON

When it comes to co-parenting in today's world, it's important to understand what that looks like in modern society. Some people believe that co-parenting should be a 50/50 split of responsibilities between the mother and father, both financially and in terms of raising the children, contributing equally to their growth and development. But if we're being realistic, co-parenting in today's society often isn't a true 50/50 split.

In many cases, when the mother and father separate, the children usually end up living with the mother. This means she often takes on much of the day-to-day responsibility of managing the children and the household. The father, on the other hand, typically spends time with the children on weekends or every other weekend. The fact that the children live primarily with the mother already challenges the idea of a 50/50 arrangement.

Given this reality, it's crucial for both parents to have a clear understanding of each other's circumstances and work together to maintain a healthy relationship for the sake of their child. Co-parenting successfully requires a cooperative approach, where both parents are willing to communicate openly and support each other in their shared goal of raising their child.

Let's explore some key points on how both mother and father can work together effectively to co-parent in today's society.

#1 - Both Parents Need to Be on the Same Page

When co-parenting, it's crucial for both parents to be on the same page to ensure the child has a stable and balanced upbringing. This is especially important when the child is being raised in two different households. Depending on the child's age, they might feel a bit confused at first because the mother and father will naturally run their households differently. It's unlikely that both parents will have identical lifestyles or rules, so it's essential to work together for the child's best interest.

For example, both parents need to agree on how to discipline the child when necessary. It can't be that one parent takes on the role of disciplinarian while the other is more laid back or doesn't enforce rules. This kind of imbalance can lead to frustration for the parent who is putting in the effort and can also be confusing for the child. The child might even start to play one parent against the other, making the situation feel like a tug of war.

Both parents must put their differences aside and present a united front when making decisions about the child. This means maintaining a working relationship, no matter what personal issues may exist between them. Being on the same page doesn't mean that mother and father will agree on everything, but it does mean they must always work together towards a common goal for their child. When both parents are aligned, it prevents the child from manipulating one parent against the other and ensures that the child feels secure and supported by both parents.

#2 - Both Parents Must Respect Each Other

For co-parenting to work effectively, both parents need to have a foundation of respect. Without respect, co-parenting simply cannot function. It's essential that both parents refrain from undermining each other's parenting styles, even if they don't always agree on how things should be done. When I say respect is crucial, I mean that each parent must acknowledge and appreciate what the other has contributed to the child's upbringing, in terms of their development and the knowledge passed on to them. Neither parent should diminish the other's contributions, as doing so can be seen as disrespectful and could lead to unnecessary arguments.

Remember, co-parenting is not a competition about who has done more for the child. It's about the combined efforts of both parents in nurturing and guiding the child. It's also vital that the child observes this mutual respect between their parents. This sets an example for how they should treat others outside of the home. If a child witnesses their parents disrespecting each other, they might mistakenly believe that this behaviour is normal or acceptable. This could lead to the child mimicking such behaviour in their interactions with others, which is not healthy.

Respect between co-parents should be based on their roles as parents, rather than on personal issues. Viewing each other from a parental perspective, rather than a personal one, simplifies the co-parenting process by keeping the focus on what truly matters: the child. Personal feelings, particularly if the relationship ended badly, can complicate the co-parenting dynamic. By keeping the respect purely within the realm of parenting, both parents can work together harmoniously, free from the emotional baggage of their past relationship. The goal is to raise the child in an environment where respect is the norm, ensuring a stable and healthy upbringing.

#3 - The Child Must Be the Primary Focus

In a co-parenting relationship, it's crucial that the child remains the main priority. Unfortunately, in many co-parenting situations today, we see some mothers using the child as a tool against fathers who genuinely want to be part of their child's life. On the other hand, some fathers might become jealous if the mother moves on with someone else or start questioning her about her personal life. All of this has nothing to do with the child and only serves to shift the focus away from what really matters.

This kind of behaviour isn't helpful when trying to co-parent effectively. Both parents need to maintain a level of discipline and maturity to ensure the focus stays on the child. There will be times when the mother and father don't see eye to eye, and disagreements may arise during the co-parenting process. If arguments do occur, it's essential that both parents work towards a resolution that benefits the child and the co-parenting arrangement as a whole.

The key is to quickly resolve any disputes and refocus on what's important – the well-being of the child. The child should always be at the heart of every decision and action taken during the co-parenting process.

#4 - Put Personal Feelings Aside

In today's society, we often see co-parenting struggles between mothers and fathers who were once in a relationship but have now gone their separate ways. Unfortunately, it's common for these parents to develop negative feelings towards each other, almost as if they've become enemies. These lingering emotions stem from the breakup and can make co-parenting difficult, especially if neither parent has fully let go of their hurt.

Breakups are never easy, particularly after years of being together, and starting over can be challenging. However, when children are involved, holding onto personal grievances can harm the co-parenting relationship and, ultimately, the child.

To foster a healthy co-parenting relationship, both parents need to set aside their personal feelings and focus on what's best for the child. In the early stages of a breakup, emotions are naturally raw, so it's important for both parents to take time to heal and process their feelings. This healing process is crucial in helping both parents move past their hurt and work together in raising their child in a balanced and supportive environment.

By addressing their emotional wounds and prioritising the child's well-being, both parents can create a more harmonious co-parenting relationship.

How to Minimise Problems During the Co-Parenting Process in Today's World

We all know that co-parenting isn't easy, especially in today's society where there are countless obstacles to navigate. It can be particularly challenging if both parents aren't getting along or find it difficult to remain civil with each other. Despite these challenges, it's essential for both parents to do whatever they can to minimise any potential problems, keeping the co-parenting relationship smooth and free from unnecessary complications. Let's explore a few ways to help minimise issues during the co-parenting process.

(i) Set Clear Boundaries with Each Other

Setting boundaries is crucial in making the co-parenting process work effectively. One of the most important boundaries that should be established is that both parents must avoid having sex with each other. Engaging in sexual relations while trying to co-parent only complicates things. If there's no intention of rekindling a serious relationship, there's no reason for either parent to continue a sexual relationship. Often, this type of interaction happens out of convenience and familiarity. The mother might still feel emotionally connected to the father, which can make the situation more complex. If the father suddenly decides to stop having sex, the mother might feel rejected and used. This can lead to her questioning his actions and assuming he is involved with someone else, triggering emotional responses that lack rationality.

In some cases, the mother might even attempt to prevent the father from seeing their child out of hurt and anger. While this may seem like an immature reaction, it's a reality in many co-parenting situations where boundaries aren't respected. Ultimately, no one benefits from this situation. The child loses out because they become caught in the conflict between their parents and are emotionally affected by it. The parents also lose because their focus shifts away from the child and onto their own hurt feelings, leading to a breakdown in the co-parenting relationship.

This is why setting boundaries is essential in a co-parenting relationship. However, it's important that these boundaries are not set for selfish reasons or personal gain. They should align with the guidelines of co-parenting that serve the best interests of the child. Clear, respectful boundaries can help maintain a healthy co-parenting relationship and ensure that the child's wellbeing remains the top priority.

(ii) Parents Shouldn't Speak Negatively About Each Other Around the Children

When parents separate, it's not uncommon for them to say negative things about each other. Unfortunately, this sometimes happens in front of the child, which is something both parents should avoid. Speaking negatively about each other in front of the child can create the impression that the parents don't like each other, even if it's just frustration being expressed. Because children are young and may not fully grasp the context of what's being said, they can easily misunderstand the situation.

If a child starts to believe that their parents dislike each other, it can create a difficult situation where they feel torn between the two. This is not a position any child should be put in; they should feel free to love and embrace both parents without the pressure of choosing sides. It's important for parents to keep their negative feelings about each other away from their children, ensuring that the child can maintain healthy, positive relationships with both parents.

(iii) Avoid Competing with Each Other in the Co-Parenting Process

In the co-parenting journey, it's important for both parents to recognise and appreciate each other's contributions to raising their child. When both parents support each other's efforts, it fosters a positive and healthy co-parenting relationship. Unfortunately, in some co-parenting situations, there's a tendency for parents to compete with each other, which is detrimental to the child's well-being.

Co-parenting isn't about keeping score or trying to outdo each other in who does more for the child. When parents fall into the trap of competing, it shifts the focus from what's best for the child to a self-serving contest of one-upmanship. The child, instead of being the focus of love and care, can end up being caught in the middle of this rivalry, which is unhealthy and confusing for them.

Rather than turning co-parenting into a competition, parents should remember that their roles are equally important in the child's life. There's no need to compete because both parents bring valuable contributions to their child's upbringing. The goal should always be to work together harmoniously, putting the child's needs and happiness above any personal egos or desires to outshine each other.

(iv) Work Together, Not Against Each Other

For co-parenting to work well, both parents need to collaborate, regardless of any personal differences they might have. Think of it like working with a colleague. You may not always get along or even like them, but the job still needs to be done. It's not about personal feelings; it's about coming together to complete the task at hand. Co-parenting is much the same. Despite any tension or unresolved feelings, both parents must put those aside to focus on raising their child together.

To make co-parenting work, it helps to consider two key things:

- Are both parents willing to work together?
- Are both parents prepared to be civil to one another?

If the answer is yes to both, that forms a solid foundation for a healthy co-parenting relationship. It's important for both parents to concentrate on each other's strengths rather than dwelling on flaws. No one is perfect, and co-parenting can be challenging, but focusing on the positives can help smooth the way.

It's also crucial to avoid pointing fingers or criticising each other's personal shortcomings during the co-parenting process. Doing so can sabotage the co-parenting relationship and shift the focus away from what really matters—the well-being of the child. When conflicts arise, parents must remind themselves of what's more important: their personal feelings or the responsibility they share in raising their child.

The key message here is for both parents to work together rather than against each other, maintaining respect and civility despite any personal differences. By doing so, they can provide a stable and supportive environment for their child, rather than leaving them caught in the crossfire of their disagreements.

Together, parents can raise a strong and resilient child; divided, they risk leaving their child vulnerable.

143

ABOUT THE AUTHOR

Courtney Sharpe was born and raised in Birmingham, UK, on October 14th, 1983, to Jamaican parents. Growing up as the middle child in a family of six siblings, three brothers and three sisters, Courtney learned early on the value of staying grounded and level-headed. His keen sense of observation of the world around him shaped his understanding of society, which has become a central theme in his writing.

Courtney's journey from childhood to adulthood has been filled with rich experiences that have contributed to his depth of character and consciousness. By the age of 25, he embarked on a revolutionary journey, developing a heightened sense of awareness about the struggles faced by individuals in modern society, which he often refers to as "Babylon." His revolutionary thought process, inspired by teachings and personal experiences, flows through the pages of his writing, offering insights and guidance for those navigating life's complexities.

Driven by a deep mission to uplift those who find it difficult to navigate through Babylon's challenges, Courtney's work speaks to the everyday struggler, offering wisdom, clarity, and empowerment. His writing is not just about survival but about overcoming and thriving, with a revolutionary spirit that challenges the status quo.

Courtney Sharpe continues to write with purpose and passion, aiming to inspire and bring about change, one reader at a time.